To Guillo

The Harmony Of Love

Bob Larzelere, M.D.

Context Publications
San Francisco

ISBN 0-932654-03-7

Library of Congress Catalog Card Number:

81-3189

Printed in the United States of America

Acknowledgements

I want to acknowledge these particular influences and forces in my life which have greatly contributed, in their own way, to the content of this book. In a time sequence, they are:

The est Training
The transcribed books and talks by Seth, as channeled and published by Jane Roberts
Two books of Richard Bach: *Jonathan Livingston Seagull* and *Illusions*
The series of books by Carlos Castaneda on the teachings of Don Juan, especially *Tales of Power*
And most recently, my direct personal and public work with Lazaris, and Peny, Michaell, and Jach of *Concept: Synergy,* the origin of many of the concepts I have used and written herein.

My thanks go to Sylvia Douglas whose friendship and typing ability produced the original manuscript.

Finally I salute Cosette Thompson and Ron Smothermon of Context Publications who worked with tireless devotion to bring this book to you.

". . . But if in your fear you would seek only
love's peace and love's pleasure,
   Then it is better for you that you cover
your nakedness and pass out of love's
threshing-floor,
   Into the seasonless world where you
shall laugh, but not all of your laughter,
and weep, but not all of your tears . . ."

The Prophet
Kahlil Gibran

The weekend before it happened had an unreal quality; it was my weekend off from a busy medical practice, and as usual, we had spent much of it on the boat. It was unusual that we had had no guests, except on Saturday when some fellow boaters stopped by for coffee or a drink. I had bought an external TV antenna for the Geru IV, our 42-foot Hatteras, because Jamie always got furious at the waxing and waning clarity of the picture, especially when we were tied up in the harbor.

While installing it on the cockpit overhead I cracked the fiberglass, cut my right thumb, and sprained my neck; I made sure Jamie heard my explosions of profanity. After all, if it were not for trying to please him—I was doing this for him—I would not have damaged myself, and I had some kind of sadistic delight in his knowing what agony I went through trying to keep him happy. He withdrew into silence.

That evening we drank ourselves to sleep—not unusual.

Sunday morning was a warm, nearly flat, calm day, typical of early November in the Bay Area. The San Francisco skyline was soft and transparent; an imaginary city floating on some distant island. Not much fun for the sailboaters, but fine for gouging massive wakes by us powerboaters. It was Sunday that I noticed a change in Jamie. Instead of talking a lot, or bitching, or being sullen, there was an unusual calm about him. His voice came from some faraway place; he almost never looked at me; and when I could really see his eyes, there was nobody home; he simply was not there.

I was puzzled, and at the same time it seemed a change for the better. He was accommodating and agreeable. I was not sensitive enough then to recognize that he was in a state of automaticity. Drinking martinis and bourbon did not affect him and I became even more suspicious when we took a ride on the bay. I asked him to plot some courses and give me the corrected compass headings.

"What heading now, Jamie?"

"Uh . . . one-seven-three."

"Something's wrong—that's almost a hundred and eighty off from our heading now."

"OK. Maybe I did it wrong. Let's see—yup, I didn't read the protractor right."

A little later, a similar mistaken heading, so I gave up. Here was Jamie, seemingly calm but suddenly unable to do simple arithmetic. I became terrified—of what I did not know. Fear gripped my body and I felt cold inside.

My hands shook on the wheel, my teeth chattered, and the fiberglass deck was vibrating not only from the twin diesels, but had the additional vibration of my entire body. The sun was shining through a beautiful haze, the bay was flat and calm, the temperature balmy, the engines were running smoothly; other boaters were enjoying the day—a normal Indian summer day.

We spoke very little, returned to the dock, washed down the boat, and drove home in silence. We drank some bourbon and went to bed separately. I noticed a gallon of vodka, unopened, in the liquor cabinet.

Jamie had just lost his third or fourth job in the last year, and had applied for unemployment insurance. I left him sleeping the next morning and went off to the hospital and the office. During the afternoon I called him. His voice was calm but distant; he said he had put together a penny-saving casserole for dinner, and asked when I would be home.

When I got home that evening, Jamie was up and about, very quiet; he seemed coordinated but incredibly unreal. The cold, clawing terror re-announced itself in my body. I had some bourbon and water; we ate some of the casserole, mostly in silence, and cleared up the dishes. I noticed that the gallon bottle of vodka had only a half-inch in the bottom.

We were in the twenty-second year of what seemed to be a

good relationship. I had met Jamie between my freshman and sophomore years in medical school, when I was looking for someone to love, to love me, and live with, so that playing the field would not be an issue during my medical training. I needed him—or someone—desperately.

On that last night, Jamie slumped into a chair to watch TV while I did some navigation work for a course I was taking. Soon, he said he was going to bed, went downstairs without a passing kiss, as I went on working. After two hours of work, I became aware of a strange, rhythmic gutteral sound coming from downstairs. I do not know how long it had been going on. I went downstairs, saw Jamie lying on his back, snoring, but not in his usual manner. It was the sound I had heard earlier that day when a man who had had surgery died from a blood clot to his lungs before recovering from anesthesia. Jamie was breathing like that: shallow and rapid, with long pauses in between. I touched him. His skin was as icy cold and wet as the sensation in the pit of my stomach.

Suddenly I remembered I had left a bottle of fifty sleeping pills out on a shelf in the living room. I ran upstairs to find it, but it was gone. I searched for the bottle indoors and out, and never found it. By the time I got back to Jamie, he had no pulse and his breathing had nearly stopped. I waited until it stopped completely.

Jamie was gone.

My terror subsided and was replaced by huge convulsive sobs of deepest grief. And at the same time there was a distinct, very real awareness of release and relief. I did not know until later that what I was experiencing was a release from our mutual prison—a prison based on need, denial, lying, emotional dishonesty, tons of buried resentment, regret, frustration, guilt, and suppressed rage and fear. Suicide, symbolic or literal, appeared to be the only way out, and Jamie took it. I was 48 years old then, and Jamie was 50. The coroner diagnosed "accidental overdose of alcohol and barbiturates, and coronary artery insufficiency, with possible myocardial infarction." I knew it was not accidental; that the real cause of his death was a broken heart.

A SYMPHONY OF ACTION
IN 12 CHAPTERS

I.
Introduction

I cannot tell you the Truth, no one can. The words in a book are only symbols of symbols which allow you to erect structures from which you may see a glimpse or a full view of the Truth. I look at words and the ideas and concepts they form as stairs one can use to ascend or expand toward the Truth. If life is a process of expanding our awareness of who we are, then when you are on the third floor, you no longer need the stairs that got you there. Those stairs may be useful to others, however, and although you have no use for them, they need not be destroyed. What follows is one of my stairways.

This is not an introductory chapter. It is an essential part of the book. Since you have read this far, you may want to take a look at what is and is not ahead. This is not a "how-to" book. It will not teach you how to love or how to receive love, for you already know that. Nor is it a cataloguing of the kinds of love; that has already been done by other writers. It is not a book of inspiration, nor is it a system of beliefs.

This book is about what is true for me, the experience of being me. Only you can discover your Truth. Whether you agree or disagree with my experience of life is irrelevant. I know that the Truth has no form or way of "right being." Knowing that, it is useful to notice and be fully aware of what one agrees and disagrees with—your "right" positions and ways of "right being." If emotions are aroused, so much the better. One could say that the value of this book for you is relative to your willingness to have and own whatever feelings, emotions, body sensations, thoughts, and attitudes come up by reading these pages. You may get bored, apathetic, angry, sad, anxious, afraid, joyful, maybe even ecstatic. I have observed that coming close to telling the truth about love can unleash buried and suppressed feelings and emotions—all of which represent the major barriers to the experience of love. That does not mean that these suppressed emotions are bad, or that you should not have them.

It does mean that the suppression of any emotion automatically suppresses the experience of what has been called the ultimate emotion: love. In truth love is not an emotion. It is a space in which emotion exists. The essence of the book is perfectly expressed in the lines from THE PROPHET which serve as the frontispiece.

I use personal experiences liberally throughout the book as illustrations of the text. I have no need to tell my "story," since the core of it, the emotional core, is not essentially different from yours or anyone else's.

That weekend before Jamie's death was representative of our life together, except that by then there was no fun, and nearly no expression of caring or of love.

From the beginning of our relationship, because I "needed" him, I was afraid to express my annoyance directly to him when I was actually annoyed. There were countless times when he would not come home from work at a time we had agreed upon, or would come home drunk. Instead of expressing my anger, I would smooth it over; suppress my experience. I vividly recall actually pushing it down, being left with a hollow, helpless sensation in my upper abdomen. Then I would say something like, "Well, I'm just glad you're home . . ."

Or he would alienate a mutual friend with a temper outburst, or by being rude or insulting, or sulking. Then instead of expressing my outrage, I would suppress it, and to please him, would often end up agreeing with him that we should not see that person any more. At that stage I always had a sinking, sick feeling, but never knew why. We lost scores of friends out of the dishonest way I dealt with my emotions; and of course, we ended up losing each other.

Sometimes, though, my frustration and anger would build to a point of explosion. One such incident I recall was when I came home late from medical school and found him in bed with one of our friends. I exploded, but instead of really confronting him with all of my rage and fear, I quickly walked out—slamming the door. There was no place to go. I walked and ran around several blocks until my body had relaxed enough so that I could talk. I never noticed then, that after one of my outbursts, even though it had been an incomplete expression, our relationship for the next few days or weeks would go smoothly, and we would enjoy being together. I did not know that it was safe to express anger, and would not have dreamed of telling him the whole truth: that I was afraid to express anger and I suppressed both the fear and anger. And furthest from my mind was the now obvious truth that my fear and anger were actually expressions of love. Distorted, yes. But had there been no love, there would have been no fear or anger. I did not see that my infrequent outbursts were really saying, "Goddammit! Don't you know I love you?"

On that Saturday before Jamie's death, I could not even express anger directly; I did it covertly, and in a way that completely squashed any self-esteem he had left.

This is a very personal book for me, and for you. My sharing what is true for me is one step removed from the truth. If you tell another my truth, it is two steps removed: a lie. One of the paradoxes about the truth is that if it is used, it becomes a lie: a system, a concept, a belief. So the truth is not something to be, or to do, or to have. It can only be a place to come from—a space or context—that which generates and allows for thought, feelings, action, process, and experience.

Perhaps even less understandable is that the communication from a printed page is only a symbol for the real communication. The real communication is also in the spaces and pauses between words, and in what is not said. In a universe of "things" we cannot create or cause something to be without simultaneously creating that which is not it. All "things" have their opposite and no "thing" is the truth. these words are not the truth. You are the truth.

The essential conditions for the existence of a thing are that it occupies a position in time and space, and that it has limits; that is, everything else is not that thing. This is a page in the book because it occupies a position in time and space, and it is surrounded by that which is not it. Words, thoughts, concepts, ideas are things.

We are all in direct communication at all times, and so this book is simply the physical symbol of a communication which has already been "broadcast" on the network which joins each of us.

Unless one can get underneath or around and see where an author is coming from, then reading a book becomes just a review of opinions, points of view, and "facts" peculiar to the author, and the real message does not come through. So what I am up to now is a kind of stage-setting, or space-creating, which will help you to see where I am coming from, rather than to have all your attention on the content of the book. The content is actually worthless. The "story" does not mean anything in itself.

This book is not written to be understood on first reading. Some of it is not understandable, only knowable.

It may be, could very well be, a book you do not want to read, for it is "love's threshing floor". Most of what we want comes from fantasies and thoughts about being comfortable. The path to the full experience and expression of love is not comfortable. And yet, it is one that everyone will sooner or later have to take. The alternative is to spend countless lifetimes in physical incarnations with suffering far greater than that imposed by the path to love and responsibility. We have already spent countless lifetimes not confronting love and responsibility.

I said that it is not about "how" and that is accurate. It is, at the same time, a very practical book. Reading these pages will not be worth much to you if you read it passively. I have written it to engage you—to interact with you—the real you, not your opinions, beliefs or tastes. The more you allow yourself to get into it—react with it—struggle with it—be skeptical of it— even defame it—the better.

It has been said that all of us are teachers and students at the same time, and that we teach what we most need to learn. I had a direct experience of that in rough-typing this manuscript from the hand-written original. As I typed, the book began to speak to me. Sometimes the telephone would ring and the caller would bring up a problem that could be resolved by something I had just typed. I was also actually watching the effects of my own belief structures and emotional suppression in an intimate relationship which started on the third day of writing the book. Opportunities arose for me to experience huge amounts of suppressed grief and fear, for example, which I had never allowed myself to express before. The cathartic effect of that alone has been of such value to me in terms of experiencing a full flow of love, that I got my money's worth and then some.

I saw that I had been so busy during the last few years showing others the way to experience love and responsibility, that I had not put to use the lessons I was teaching.

Here is a suggestion: the space between the ends of a chapter and the beginnings of the next is purposeful. I suggest you let some time lapse—an hour, a day, or more, between chapters.

II.
Contact with a New Reality

One of the areas I decided very early to explore during this life was that of love. I have used this life as a kind of field test or laboratory, if you will, to experience the range of love: from that with all kinds of conditionality, need, and attachment, to that of completely unconditional, no strings attached love. Most of us, perhaps all, have been involved in the conditional form of love. If you had parents, it is safe to say that very early on you learned and practiced love with conditions. This is not a slur against parents. It is a statement of what each of us thought we had to do in order to survive as infants or very young children.

I recall when I realized that I no longer needed my parents. I was twenty-two, in the Army, knew I was going to to study medicine after the Second World War, and had my first intimate sexual experiences. What I did not notice then was that I had transferred needing my parents to needing others. And I kept looking for someone who would fulfill my need. I met Jamie some years later and it appeared my longing was answered. I was 26 and he was 28. The condition of love which I kept firmly in place was that the person I loved filled my need for comfort, security, companionship, a place to dump my troubles, and most of all, sexual gratification. I had sex so linked with the expression of love, that when it was not available, I literally felt unloved and unwanted. I clearly had physical intimacy and orgasm as a condition for giving or receiving love.

When I met Jamie he was working, with a good salary. I was in medical school, and later in internship and residencies, with a mere subsistence salary and my parents contributing heavily to my financial support. Dad had always hoped and prayed that I would become a doctor; and when, toward the end of my senior year in music school, I awoke one morning about three, sat straight up in bed, suddenly knowing that after the War I would go to medical school, he was overjoyed.

For me, the person I needed was Jamie. After the years of post-graduate training, and then starting in practice in partnership with an older physician who was devoted to me and my success, there came a time when I was making more money than Jamie. When I looked back later, I could see that as the beginning of the decline of our relationship. You see, IF YOU THINK YOU REALLY NEED SOMEONE, THE WAY YOU KEEP THAT PERSON AROUND IS TO MANIPULATE THEM SO THAT YOU GET THEM TO NEED YOU. I did that masterfully. From that point on, it was all my show. I was the one who decided on the next expensive boat, on building a house, on who we entertained and how, on which trips to take. If Jamie objected, I would override him, or sulk or cajole, until I got my way. I was beginning the process of getting him under my control.

It was as though my sense of being OK depended on keeping him in my prison no matter what the cost to his self-respect and self-esteem. When he was depressed, I felt helpless. When he had a temper tantrum, especially when drunk, I was scared. When I expressed anger, he would withdraw, hurt and sullen, or would walk out. No matter how many times we said "I love you," the wounds never healed.

This is what conditional love looks like.

There is an experience of a space or context, a place to come from, which is so intimately a part of the experience of loving and being loved, that one could say the two experiences are just different facets of the same thing; or are, in fact, the same. Without being willing to experience this space, it is impossible to experience and manifest love. This space is one of ultimate responsibility: I create my own reality.

The word "reality" needs some clarification. For each of us there are two realities, only one of which is real. The reality we usually call real is the universe we perceive with our senses: what we see, hear, smell, touch, taste; the incidents, events, circumstances; our thoughts, judgements, evaluations, notions, concepts, conclusions, beliefs, etc. This reality is not real; it is constantly changing; it includes and is a function of time. It is the universe of illusionary persistence which is a function of change. I will call it the illusion-reality. It is the reality of process and organizing principles. It is the reality of dichotomies and opposites. It is silly-putty.

The reality which is real is that which cannot be talked about except in terms which come from the illusion-reality. It is the reality of cause; generating principle; power of will and imagination; that which creates and allows for all illusion-realities. It is timeless, changeless, infinite, absolute. It can only be experienced directly. It cannot be found in the world of perception. Only its effects can be witnessed. It is the reality of our imagination.

Love, emotions, and all experience dwell in this reality beyond time and place.

In the illusion-reality there is apparent cause and effect. We say that the streptococcus causes "strep" throats, and that penicillin or other antibiotics "cause" a cure. We say that because the earth rotates, we have day and night; that because a sperm penetrates an ovum, a body starts to form. It is the universe of systems, of beliefs; because we do or do not do such and such, this or that happens or does not happen. When the illusion-reality is viewed from the real reality, it is obvious that there are only effects. We are always operating in both realities, but most of the time we do not notice that we, individually and together, are the source or cause or generating principle of the illusion-reality. That state of being which allows us to see that cause is not outside the Self, some call transformation. Transformation does not occur as a result of changing attitudes or points of view. That can produce conversion to another set of organizing principles, but not transformation. Conversion is easy to spot in yourself or others. The classic example is the sinner who suddenly sees the light, reforms, and now condemns sin and sinners. There has simply been a dramatic shift to a different set of operating principles, not a transformation. The test for conversion is simple; if you are making right what you are doing now and wrong what you were doing, you have converted, not transformed. Transformation includes all dichotomies, gives freedom to choose appropriate action, and is not based on a right-wrong system motivated out of fear.

A year and a half after Jamie's death I had an experience which clearly demonstrated to me who was causing my illusion-reality, and served as a brilliant lesson in letting go—in letting life happen instead of trying to make it happen.

A San Francisco social group planned to rent three house-boats and spend the Memorial Day weekend in the Sacramento-San Joaquin delta. A member of the group who was a patient and friend of mine, knowing that I frequently boated in the delta, asked me if I would bring my boat up from the Bay to meet them and show them around for the three-day weekend. None of the group has boated in the delta before. I liked the idea, agreed to do it, and invited three guests to go with me on the Geru IV.

On the Saturday morning of the long weekend, we left the harbor in Richmond, starting the nearly fifty mile trip to our rendezvous with our friends and their houseboats. It was a day with broken clouds; some sun, some shade, and little showers now and then.

I had both studied and taught small boat piloting and navigation as a member of the local U.S. Power Squadron and I often charted courses in good weather just to keep in practice for days of fog and low visibility. Charting a course from one point to the next, getting the true direction in degrees of that line, then converting the true direction to a compass heading. The purpose of this is to be able to navigate safely in the absence of visibility.

I decided to try an experiment: I would simply look at the chart to see the next course change, and then without plotting it or making the corrections, close my eyes and get a number. The idea was that the number would be the corrected compass heading. As we approached the Richmond-San Rafael bridge, I left the wheel, walked over to the chart table, saw the next buoy beyond the bridge. I closed my eyes, and to my surprise, got a number. When I walked back to the wheel, the compass read that number. The boat was already on the corrected heading, and I had not touched the wheel! I figured that could be a lucky accident. As we approached the buoy, I again looked at the chart, observed the next buoy, and closed my eyes. A number flashed, and I went to the wheel, and again I had not steered. Now I began to get excited. When the third course change happened in exactly the same way, I became inspired. It dawned on me that I was wasting time even looking at the chart; I said loudly and firmly to myself: "What I want to happen is, the boat will go all the way up the river without my steering it. It will follow the safest, most comfortable, most economical course, and follow all the rules of the road."

A twin-engine boat can be steered by changing relative engine speeds, so I decided not to touch the throttles except in an emergency. The route from the Bay to the delta is used by ocean-going freighters, and a channel is maintained for them. Small boats can go aground if the pilot steers away from the channel in certain areas where the depth of water goes suddenly from 30 feet to 2 or 3 feet, especially, of course, at low tide. There are many curves, bridges to go under, and many narrow channel areas. In addition to which it was Memorial Day week-end, and it looked like everyone who owned a boat was out on the water—from ski boats and small sailboats to huge sailing and power yachts.

It happened.

For the fifty miles to our rendezvous, I did not touch the wheel or change engine speed. The boat followed all the rules of the road, took obviously safe and comfortable headings. There were times, when heading for a narrow bridge opening, that the boat would veer off to starboard, not heading for the bridge at all. I would ache to grab the wheel and get it back "on course." Then, slowly, it would come back on course, and by the time we got to the bridge I could see, in retrospect, what had happened. The boat took the long curved route so that when we got to the bridge, other boats had cleared away.

What steered the boat? Well, I could tell you in part that hydrodynamically things happened: a gust of wind would push the stern around a little. An eddy or the wake of a passing boat would shift the heading. And sometimes one or the other engine would speed or slow slightly, without any change in the throttles. But what was running the mechanics of all that? It was so far beyond the realm of chance that I could not even consider that possibility. And on Monday when we returned the 50 miles to Richmond, it happened again. Two of my passenger friends saw it happen and could, with more or less strain, believe it. The third friend ignored the whole thing, did not want to hear about it even when it was happening, and was sure that the rest of us were insane.

What I was left with was that some part of me, or something of which I was a part knew how to control all the factors involved in that trip, and had been called into play because I had suspended my belief that it could not happen. That trip became a parable for me. I learned the lesson of letting go; of giving up dominating and manipulating and trying to control myself or others; of giving up that I, Bob Larzelere, knew how to make things work or have things happen. I literally stopped trying to figure out how to manipulate life.

I am going to suggest a stairway, or structure, which you can use to bring yourself closer to the experience of ultimate responsibility. I suggest that you ask yourself the question: "Am I willing to experience being the cause of my life?"

If the answer is yes, that means that you are willing to give up blaming others or yourself; willing to give up resentments, regrets, being right (and you can be right about being wrong). It would mean you would have to give up being a martyr. You would have to give up your games of manipulation and domination as well as the game of avoiding domination. You must be willing to be that of which you have thought yourself only a part.

In what I had said so far about the relationship with Jamie, the result of such games should be clear. Perhaps the end will not be quite so dramatic as suicide, but there will be a slow dissolution into separation at all levels of experience. I cannot now, or ever, speak for Jamie; but I can speak for my experience of him in the light of what I know now about my responsibility for the failure of our relationship. From the very beginning of our time together, I dominated him. I was smarter, more educated; and eventually had more money. I almost always got my way even knowing that it hurt him in the only place we can damage others: his self-esteem. My survival act was to dominate him in order to avoid being dominated; his was to be dominated, using me as the excuse for his suffering. I was just as much the victim, however.

There are two ways to play victim: resist, or succumb. I resisted being a victim, which meant that I unwittingly became the victim of not being dominated by Jamie. I had no choice. I had to resist his domination. Jamie chose to succumb, and on the surface he gave in to my domination, but at the same time he completely controlled me. When I won and he lost, I would get sick, or depressed. When he won, and he did sometimes, I would feel threatened because my battle plan had failed. I did not know then that I was getting exactly what I intended so that I could discover and experience what does not work in human relationships.

Later, as my experience grew of being responsible for and being cause of my life, including the people in it and all the circumstances, I could see that he never really did anything to me that I was not allowing to happen. There was not anything to forgive him for! I could only forgive myself. After that, all resentments and regret disappeared.

If giving up being a victim and giving up dominating and avoiding domination looks like too much for you right now, here is a simpler stairway: see if you are willing to pretend—just pretend—at least while reading this book, that you are the cause of your reality. You do not have to believe it, or agree with it, or experience it. Just see (if the experience of love is important to you) if you are willing to pretend, like a game, that you cause your illusion-reality—all of it—the good and the bad. If you are willing to play this game with yourself, proceed. If not, I suggest you stop reading this until you are ready to play life in this way. Do not wait too long—life will pass you by.

There is good evidence that, within the next few years, the master physicists of the world will present incontrovertible proof that our illusion-reality exists because we think it into existence, and all that stuff we call soft or hard is made of nothing. It is no more real than the pictures we see in the movies or on TV: a light show made out of trapped and reflected light, a hologram. And the writers, directors, film makers, projectionists, and projectors of this light show? You and me.

Each of us is watching a different movie with enough similarity of the props (by agreement) that it appears we are on the same set. We are not.

To go back to the beginning of this chapter: I realized a few years ago, that as my experience of taking responsibility for all aspects of my life expanded, my experience of loving and being loved also expanded. I saw that self-esteem and self-love were functions of responsibility. As blame, guilt, resentment and regret dropped away, I began to respect and esteem myself and others more. And the love that was always there was revealed.

Love exists in the real reality. It is absolute, meaning that it has no opposite. It manifests and expresses itself in the illusion-reality where it appears to have oppositions. One way of describing what is going on in the world could be this: there are only two things going on, only one of which is real. The two things going on are:

1. Love, and

2. The barriers to the experience and expression of love.

Love is real. The barriers are illusions. The illusion-reality is a manifestation of our thoughts and beliefs—our frozen thoughts.

The rest of this book deals with melting and dissolving that which is illusion.

III.
Everyday Miracles

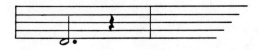

By now you may have realized that this is not about spoon-feeding you to become part of some soupy porridge to swoon into—into a state of eternal bliss and universal love, a cosmic sea of ecstasy. That is where we come from; that is where we already are and always will be. And it is a grossly inadequate way of talking about that which we cannot talk about. Yes, we can experience that cosmic sea, but our language cannot hold anything more than a pale symbol or concept of that experience.

I cannot describe or define love; and if you are honest with yourself, you will see that the best we can do is to describe its manifestations, its expressions, and its qualities in the illusion-reality. Love is not a thing. It is an absolute. It does not have a position in time or space, nor is there that which is not it.

I have, so far, drawn a bleak picture of that 22-year long relationship with Jamie. There were also wonderful times when we loved being together and when we could share that joy with others. Those times seemed to be invalidated by some of the horrors. But when I look back, I see that the firm foundation of our relationship came from love. Even the horrors were expressions of love, distorted, and sometimes unrecognizable. The worst part was the deep frustration of not knowing how to have it work or to make it work. When I finally knew that I did not know what to do or how, I found out. But long after he had died.

It is useful for me, and it may be for you, to view love as though we experience it in octaves: the octaves of musical scales. And to stretch the analogy further, it includes all the overtone series of each note in each octave. For example: the first octave is love at the level of security; the second octave is love at the feeling and sensory level. Third is love at the level of emotions; it is also using love to manipulate another; the child, about age four, discovers how he or she can manipulate to get mother's love. The fourth octave contains conditional self love in its lower register and unconditional love of self in its upper. The fifth octave is loving beyond yourself—loving others—loving one's self first, then others. The sixth octave is love of humanity, and the seventh, cosmic love. It is impossible to love another fully until love of self is as shining and clear as the deep tones of the lowest octave of the harp.

Each of us varies, uniquely, in the number of octaves in which we send out our music, our vibrating energy, as well as the development of each of the seven notes in each octave, and the quality and strength of the overtone series of each note. One could say, then, that to the degree I have undeveloped octaves, or undeveloped or out of tune notes within any given octave, I cannot respond to another who is sending out music in ranges in which I am unable to resonate. The decibel level then, between two or more people will vary from silence to full volume, and from total dissonance to total harmony. As one opens up to letting in another's music, harmonies are formed which complete what seemed to be missing in each person alone. The dissonances may be held as exciting and fun and as opportunities to work out their resolution to harmony, or as barriers. When held as barriers, self-invalidation and invalidation of the other person occur, leading to more dissonance.

When two people get together who have similarly well-developed octaves as well as four or five or more such octaves, pure magic happens. It is as though there is a piling up of those octaves such that a single note from one person will resonate through many octaves in the other, and one or more overtones will become the fundamental note for another overtone series. One can see how poetry, music, sculpture, and painting come into being as attempts to communicate this magic. In addition to the resonance, two people can produce a music far beyond the simple addition of one group of notes to another group. When two people resonate completely, there is an awakening effect on other people.

Beneath all of this, as an eternal organ-point, is that one tone, that one spark of consciousness, which not only unites us all, but is that original energy which is our Source: timeless, infinite, forever creating new harmonies and dissonances for the pure joy of creation out of love.

When you reach that original tone, every cell in your body will celebrate, singing in a real physical experience of ecstasy rarely known in the history of the human race. That is available to you, and it begins to happen when you and I decide to love the dissonances, and take delight in finding ways to harmonize them. Then we develop more notes and more octaves and more overtones, all in tune with the original tone of creation.

It is possible, even probable, that if being human has a reason, it is to learn the lessons of love, expressed humanly. Not to dream of our origin and desire to return to that nirvana or heaven or whatever, but to create the experience of unconditional love while here, now, in bodies. In fact, that potential of the body as a vehicle through which we express our godliness has barely been tapped. There have always been a few individuals in each age who achieve the maximal power of the body to express, and they have served as reminders of the potential available to all of us.

I do not intend to imply that there are goals or ends to

achieve. There are only means and no ends. If what we call goals or ends are not means to further transcendence, transformation, and creativity, then they are worthless. For me there is no goal of a heaven or nirvana where all desire ceases, for that would be ultimate hell. What we are as living beings is the incredible desire to create and express. We are the expression itself, and we are endlessly expanding, transcending, creating and expressing. There are no ends, only means. Life's experiences (such as my boat trip) are not an end or a goal. They become the means for a further expansion into responsibility, of further divesting ourselves from being the victims of our environment. They are a further expansion of the awareness of who we are and what we are up to here in our small corner of this universe.

Love, creativity, desire, expression, and participation are such functions of each other that we can hold them only as our illusion-reality categorizations of the same transcendental experience: the experience of Self, of communion with my higher consciousness; of our oneness with Source. We are one and many at the same time.

So it is not possible to consider love without also considering creativity, the desire to express, expression itself, and participation—the ultimate expression of love.

Love is active. It thrusts out. It is aggressive. It does not suppress itself, nor will it be suppressed. It may show itself in bizarre and deformed ways when we withhold it or when we refuse to receive it from others. These distortions of love manifest as hate, hostility, anger, grief, fear, apathy, and all their variations including jealousy, invulnerability, resentment, rejection, illness, and death. Beneath all these and many other describable distortions, one always finds love seeking expression, and the need for being loved.

If being in the space of love is our natural state, how did we make such a mess of it? It is useful to tell yourself the truth about the experience and expression of love in your daily living right now. Not just your capacity to express and receive, but also that of those around. If you look at your life honestly, you will begin to notice that the people around you have remarkable reflective qualities. What I mean is that your immediate environment of people reflect your own barriers to the experience of love. That is not good news to most. Remember: "I create my own reality." Whatever is going on in your personal interior environment will be reflected back at you from your macrocosmic environment whether you are aware of that or not. I ask you to become aware of it.

Before looking at other people, it may be easier to start with your own body. Your body will always be absolutely honest with you. To whatever degree you are blocking the expression of love — to or from others — your body will tell you with pains, soreness, fatigue, injuries, and disease states. Your body is a miraculous tool to remind you of whatever it is you have not taken responsibility for. Suppressed emotions, including love, blame and guilt, resentment, and regret, will always manifest as a symptom or syndrome in your body. For some this has been so unendurable they have suppressed all feeling and emotion, and are literally walking around in apathy, with "dead" bodies.

The messages from your body to you are in code and the code is not difficult to crack once you are willing to accept the notion that your body (more accurately, your higher consciousness through your body) is trying to tell you something. The simplest way to find out what the message is, is to ask your body. For this to work, you must suspend disbelief. It takes a little practice to "hear" the answer, but the answer comes to you often in a form you would not expect — something someone else says, something you read by chance, a dream, sometimes in direct words from somewhere inside or outside you. This has miraculous practical value in getting to and eliminating the source of disease.

Around the time of the weekend boat trip, I saw that since we create our own realities through our beliefs, then all illness must be created out of our own considerations or beliefs.

Since I was practicing medicine then, I decided to find out what kind of practical value this might have. I discussed this idea with some of my patients whom I thought would be open to such a farout idea, and I made some mistakes in choosing people to discuss it with. The discussion angered or scared the hell out of a few people, and only later could I see why. They came to a doctor to see a doctor, not to listen to someone with a new theory. I wisely, but not completely, bridled my enthusiasm.

Some of my patients were very open. One of the first was a woman in her seventies who had a several-year history of low back pain due to the demineralization and softening process of the spine which sometimes occurs in women after menopause. She had had back braces, pain killers including codeine, and hormones, but the pain continued. She had resigned herself to very limited activity since even walking aggravated the pain. The only requirement for getting to her belief or consideration, was our mutual agreement that there was such a consideration, and that it was the source of her disability. We both knew that the bone-softening was the justification or explanation of her disability, not the cause.

We had two short visits, and in the second she saw that the pain had started when she was involved in a love triangle as the "other woman." When we looked at each flare-up of pain, even several times during a day, we found that it was always just after a thought about being the "other woman." Her consideration was that she had to be punished for such behavior. She punished herself with a symbolic stab in the back. When she saw that, the pain disappeared, and did not return. She was able to resume an active life.

I tend to recall these early examples most vividly since they were so exciting for me and the patients who benefited. Later, such miracles became commonplace.

An even more dramatic example happened about the same time with a young school teacher whom I will call Helen. Helen was a close friend as well as a patient: warm, open, loving, a joy to be around. She was petite, pretty, and attractive. Two to four times each year she would have severe streptococcus infections in her throat. This always required penicillin and two or more days of being too sick to leave her home.

She was willing to do anything to reduce these strept-throats, and when she came in with a fever of 102°, tonsils in-flamed and swollen to the point of meeting in the midline of her throat, with enlarged, tender lymph nodes in her neck, I said, "Helen, I'll take a throat culture as usual right now, but if you'd like I'll hold off on the penicillin until later today. Can you come back about five this afternoon? We'll see if we can get to the source of it."

She agreed, and came back about two hours later, at five. We started. And we got it! It was: "I'm too small."

When we looked back at every sore throat she could re-member, each was preceded by the thought, "I'm too small." The "small" could refer to her physical size, her mental or emo-tional state, smallness about anything.

I could not believe my eyes. When she uncovered that hid-den belief, she suddenly looked well. Her skin changed from sal-low gray to radiant aliveness. I took her into the examining room and looked in her throat. It was normal! The tonsils were normal size and healthy. The swollen lymph nodes in her neck had disappeared. She felt great. Her temperature was 98.5°. That was the last sore throat she had for the next six years.

I could not report such results in a medical journal. It lacked proof. Only Helen and I knew what had happened. Even before and after photographs would not be believed. I had learned nothing about such things in medical school, or any post-graduate medical course.

The only common denominators in those two dramatic examples, as well as the host of subsequent releases from illness, were that I was there when it happened, and both the patient and I were willing to be responsible for creating our illusion-reality, rather than blaming it on a thousand and one external factors and circumstances.

It is not always easy to give up the consideration or belief that is uncovered. One has such a belief because it provides some payoff in the area of avoiding responsibility; blame, guilt, avoidance and fear of impact; or the debilitating self-pity of "If only . . . I would have been happy;" and the most devastating payoff of all: the ego's insistence on its own importance which is expressed as the attitude of "better than." I have seen people who would rather die than to give up blaming a mother, father, husband, or wife. And they died, unforgiving, for they could not forgive themselves. I am not saying that this is bad or wrong or should not exist. I am just saying that it is so—that sometimes people die rather than give up a belief.

The most annoying and unrelenting physical syndrome I have had persisted over a ten year period. It started at a time when Jamie and I started to taking moving pictures as a hobby. I bought a Bolex 16mm camera and an expensive Bolex projector, and we were off on another descending spiral of domination and submission. I said it was "our" camera, but I made sure I was always in control.

One day I was lying on my stomach in the yard for a long time, taking pictures of our two Siamese cats interacting with some birds. That evening my neck was sore, and by the next morning my neck was rigid with pain just to the right of the cervical spine. I also had pain going down my right arm ending with a painful sensitive numbness in my little finger. It was so severe that I immediately arranged to see my favorite orthopedist that morning. When he examined me, he told me, as I expected, that there was pressure on a nerve in my neck, that a cortisone injection might help, a soft cervical collar would be necessary, and he arranged for x-rays. The vertebrae of my neck by x-ray looked as though a powerful egg-beater had chewed its ways from my shoulders to my head. The orthopedist and I knew that meant I could look forward to years of problems, since that kind of arthritis is not medically or surgically correctible. So sure enough, and to spare you the details, I was very careful with my neck (which made it worse), sometimes used cervical traction in bed at home (some relief), had occasional physical therapy with deep heat and gentle traction (which helped), and wore soft and hard cervical collars when it was at its worst. There were long periods when I had no problems, and I would hope that it would not return, but it always did.

Then Jamie died, and Jamie II came along (next chapter) and my neck problems became much worse. One morning three weeks before the boat trip, I awoke with neck pain turned on full blast. I was in San Francisco, and had to drive home to Ber-

keley, and I did not know whether I could or not. I did. On the way a voice suddenly said in my head: "SO THINGS AREN'T GOING THE WAY YOU WANT THEM TO ARE THEY?"

In a flash I saw what my life had been about up to that moment: trying to change people so that they would be the way I thought they should be; dominating, not noticing I was the one being dominated by the compulsion to have it all my way.

In that instant every cubic inch of the pain turned off as though a switch had suddenly been flipped to "off." In the nine years since then my neck problem never returned. There has not been even a suggestion of it.

When I was in the seventh grade, age twelve, puberty happened. I fell in love with my best friend who had recently moved
to the small Kansas town where I grew up. That one-sided being
in love went on for over ten years, and I knew all along how it
would end. He would marry and have children, and I would go
on loving him anyway, all of which happened. That year I discovered that I could not see writing on the blackboard unless I
sat in the front of the room. When a school nurse came around
to test vision, I felt humiliated to find out that I was near-sighted
and would need glasses. I knew Dad would be furious that a son
of his would have less than the perfect vision he had. He was,
but agreed that I should go to the best eye doctor in the area and
be checked. I came home with glasses.

Also that same year the musical ROBERTA opened, and
the best known song, at least then, was one my mother loved to
sing (she had a voice like Flagstad), and I would accompany her
on the piano when she sang it at home or in public. The eye
doctor said my vision would probably get worse during my teen
years, and it did, then did not change much during adulthood,
until . . .

Not long after the neck problem had vanished, I decided to
see what belief was holding my myopia in place. In looking for
it, I saw in my mind's eye, visions of all kinds of people with no
eyes, blind eyes, dark glasses, and in the background there was
music. I suddenly recognized the music and the words:

"They said someday you'll find
 All who love are blind;
 When your heart's on fire, you must realize
 Smoke gets in your eyes."

I recall laughing for the next three days. My vision nearly
cleared up, enough so that I no longer had to wear my glasses
except at night driving in the rain. I had bought, hook, line, and

sinker, the words to that song when I was in love the first time. There were other considerations too, like not wanting to look ahead too far into the future, and getting even with my Dad for something or the other.

So that is the way it works. I will present you with more personal examples later.

To whatever degree we block the inflow and outflow of love, our bodies tell us, and so do our closest, and not so close, associates: the people we live with, work with, and deal with on a daily basis. Does a salesperson snap at you? Look to see what you are suppressing. Does your boss ignore you and not acknowledge you? Look to see who you ignore and fail to acknowledge. Are people starving in the world? The existence of hunger and starvation in the world represents our individual starvation for love and self-esteem and our individual failure to take responsibility for the realities we create. At a basic fundamental level, by not loving ourselves, we create, unconsciously, suffering in the world.

So far, I have only hinted at what the barriers are to the full experience of love. In the remaining chapters, we will delve into them and see how to dissolve them. Remember: barriers exist only in the reality which is created by thought. There are no naturally occuring barriers in life.

IV.
Loving Beyond Manipulation

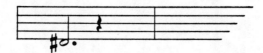

Here is a reminder: everything I have said and will say in this book is what is true for me right now. I do not mean to say that it should be true for you. At any moment what is true for me now may change. If you make beliefs or systems out of what I say, you will risk delaying your process toward expanding your awareness of Self. And it is alright to do that. You have to find out what works and does not work for yourself by direct observation. So, from here on, I will not qualify statements with an "as I see it . . ." or a "what is true for me is . . .". That will be understood. So given that, regarding love . . .

The barriers or blockages fall into two broad categories:

1. Threats to survival,

2. Emotion which has been suppressed, limited, held back, disowned, feared—in other words, emotion which has not been allowed to flow outward and be eliminated.

Categorizing the barriers in that way should raise some questions. It is useful to stop here, re-read the paragraph above, and simply look at the questions or comments you have. Have a discussion with yourself.

You and I set up problems for ourselves to learn from. And each problem provides us with the opportunity to become personally responsible for creating our reality exactly the way it is. If we refuse the experience of responsibility, the problem repeats itself later in time, often with different scenery, different characters, and the roles are the same. Only the names and the costumes change, and there is a compulsion to repeat your problem patterns. When we finally look at a problem from the point of view of being the cause of it instead of being the effect of it, we receive the gift of self-esteem and love.

Less than three months after Jamie's death, I met Jamie II. His actual name was the same as Jamie I's actual name. He came aboard the boat as the guest of one of Jamie's oldest friends from their days in the Navy together. There was instant attraction, and I had been lonely. I did not notice then that I picked up with Jamie II about where I had left off with Jamie I. Jamie II was already out of a job, already depressed, already drank heavily (as did I), and what was worse, already needed me. Much of our time together, perhaps most, was spent in either being drunk at the same time, or being hung-over.

I had an unusual warning, which I ignored, and only later saw its significance. Jamie II was younger than I was, and looked even younger than his actual age. One afternoon on the way to the boat I stopped at a liquor store to buy a bottle of Scotch for him. Just as the clerk was handing me the bottle, there was a tremendous crash in the rear left corner of the store, and both the clerk and I looked back and saw first a hole in the ceiling, then a clothed body lying in a pile of broken bottles and spilled wine. Before we could move, the person got up and walked shakily up to the front. It was a young boy who was working at the store. He had gone to the second floor, tripped, and fell through the ceiling at a point where there was no floor. He was shaken, frightened, but had no physical damage—not even cuts from the broken glass. He even looked a little like Jamie II. I ignored this providential warning. One of the main reasons I was buying Scotch was that Jamie II was much more affectionate and open to physical intimacy when he had been drinking. And even so, I was still blind to the obvious damage I was doing to him by making sure we had liquor on hand so that I could fill my need for intimacy.

Our relationship and our lives went from deteriorated to more deteriorated. About a year later, in an early morning outburst of my rage and frustration, I left him. I did not call him.

A month later he called me and said he had something important to talk to me about and that talk resulted in my personal transformation. I was able for the first time to experience responsibility for, to experience being the cause of, both relationships. I do not mean that I blamed myself, felt guilt, despair, or resentment—just simply, the experience of "I caused all this," and with both partners, who out of love for me, played their roles in my drama perfectly. It was out of the relationship with Jamie II that I discovered one of the most liberating truths about me: that my alrightness, self-respect, experience of loving and being loved did not depend upon sexual intimacy. That does not mean that I then made sex wrong, or swore it off; it meant that I no longer was compelled to have sex to prove my self-worth. My self-worth was beginning to come from internal sources instead of from external validation. I was free! There is no way to acknowledge Jamie II enough for providing me with the opportunity to discover that freedom. We remain close friends.

About a year ago I realized that I was in a new, expanded space with respect to love. I woke up one morning and saw that for the first time in my life, I was experiencing the ability to love in an unconditional way. It had come about from an experience of loving another completely, including physically intimate expression, and I was not attached! There was no need in it. No yearning to be with. No sorrow at parting. No jealousy. If we would never be together again there would be no loss. It was complete. And my experience of loving others soared.

I saw that for the last six years, I had avoided, not altogether consciously, the expression of love intimately, physically. I had a lurking fear of once again needing, becoming hooked, of love becoming conditional. There are many ways to manifest and express love: in creating activity, in work. And my job was one perfectly suited to the giving and receiving of love without physical or sexual intimacy. I had a direct experience of the variety of legitimate ways love can be expressed. But I woke up that morning to an open door—which I had opened to a space of love without conditions or strings. That space continues to expand.

V.
The Value and Magic of Love: Jerry

I cannot describe the actual experience of unconditional love. I can only describe its effects. One of those effects resulted in an incident that spanned a number of weeks last summer. I report the story of it in detail because what happened was for me a clear observation and experience of what can happen when love is expressed to another human being who has barriers to allowing the experience of love to flow in or out.

I have a physician friend whom I have known for three years, whom I will call Jerry. On the surface Jerry was a magnificent success: brilliant, handsome, with a successful practice, and many friends. He contributed time to serving people far beyond his medical practice. However, there was an area of his life which was unsatisfactory to him and to those close to him, having to do particularly with his relationship with his parents, and with women. He wanted to meet a woman who would become his wife, have children, and have a fulfilling family life. However it seemed that no relationship ever turned out. With respect to his parents, he vacillated between blaming them, wanting to please them, and feeling guilty when he did not please them. Since he used me as a friend, counselor, and consultant, our discussions usually centered on this aspect of his life. His use of me in that way was natural since that is what I have done professionally for a number of years, but there were no miraculous results from Jerry. No matter what I asked, said, or did, there was no transformation, no experience of true responsibility. At times he could see and acknowledge his responsibility for setting up his reality, but it would always be short-lived. No progress. Nothing happened.

One evening just after my birthday last summer, he invited me to dinner to celebrate my birthday. We made our plans for a couple weeks later and then a sudden inspiration hit me. I said, "Jerry, what I'd like to do that evening, since it's my evening, is to spend as much time as it takes to express my love for you."

He visibly, though slightly, drew back, and looked pale.

I continued, "This is actually for me, since I have never completely told another the degree and depth of my love. If you're willing, that's what I'd like to do." I wanted to get to the bottom of his difficulty with receiving love—with creating the experience of being loved.

His withdrawal and pallor increased, and he said very little during the short time we were together after that. Usually he telephoned me once or twice a week, but for the next two weeks, no calls. On the day of our dinner appointment I called his answering service. The operator told me that his beeper was not working, so I could not get in touch with him directly.

"Oh boy," I thought, "we're really out of communication."

Later he called and sounded exasperated. He blamed his secretary for not making a dinner reservation at the place he wanted to go; said we would have to drive all the way downtown; and that he would pick me up.

He did.

When I got in the car, I asked him how he was doing.

He said, "Terrible. Nothing is working. My sick patients are sicker. I'm worn out. One of my cars quit running and the mechanic can't find the problem. The books are a mess at the office. It couldn't be worse. On top of that . . ."

I interrupted, "When did all this start?"

"Two weeks ago."

"After I told you what I intended for tonight?"

"Yeah . . ."

The "yeah" sounded like it came from inside a tomb.

"You hoped I'd forget?" I asked, and went on, "I didn't forget. In fact, I'm going to start now . . ."

At this moment the engine of his car sputtered and nearly stalled. We were heading for a freeway.

Then I went on: "Look, Jerry, I want to be clear that I'm do-

ing this for me. I do not want anything from you at all. You don't have to even understand that I love you." (Engine sputter.)

". . . I do not want sex with you, I do not need you, you are not obligated to be or do anything. You are simply the person I picked to express my love to. It could be any of a large number of people I love." Another engine sputter.

When we got to the restaurant there was a police officer in front who would not let us double-park for the restaurant's valet parking service. Jerry was furious.

Driving around the block to a garage, in the middle of an intersection, I said, "I love you."

The car engine stopped cold.

It started when I laughed and said OK, I'd hold off until we were seated inside.

We were seated at a relatively private table, and ordered a fabulous French dinner. While tasting the quenelles, I said, "I love you," and he choked.

From then on, for the nearly three hours we were in the restaurant, Jerry said and did everything he could to get me to stop, except for physical violence and walking out.

He said, "You must be insane. Does anyone know you're doing this? Do you know what you're doing?"

And it got much worse. He became nasty. He covered the entire range of survival defenses from suspicion to open viciousness. Had I wanted anything from him, had I any attachment or conditions in my love for him, I probably would have given up or left him there in the restaurant. But none of his covert and overt hostility affected me, for I had no need, no attachment.

I frequently acknowledged him for his obvious willingness to go through torture in reaction to my expression of love. It was a true measure of his bigness, of his human magnificence.

Early during the dinner incident, I wondered if I were just mouthing the words, "I love you." Then I realized that I was coming from and being love itself, into which I created the communication, "I love you." When I saw that, the next "I love you" produced the most severe reaction of all. It was like a laser beam splitting his armor. He grabbed his chest, turned pale and drawn, gasped for breath, and fell forward into his entree. He turned blue. All the signs of a coronary attack.

I laughed, and said, "Jerry, knock it off—you can't frighten me that easily."

He immediately sat up and regained some composure. He was able to eat very little and remembers almost nothing about the excellent cuisine. The whole experience was, for me, as close to an exorcism as I care to be.

We finished, and he was shaken, weak, and could hardly walk. We did walk until he felt secure enough to drive, and he took me back to my hotel.

I returned home the next day, and he called once to report that everything in his life had become worse. A patient had died unexpectedly; a colleague had died of a coronary; patient referrals had hit a new low, and he could not stand being around people. I reaffirmed my experience of love for him with a simple "I love you."

Eight days after our dinner, he phoned me, and said in a vicious voice I had never heard from him, "I want you to know that I absolutely HATE you! I do not want to see you again! You have ruined my life!"

I replied lightly, "Well, Jerry, now I know you love me. I also know it's the first time in your life you have expressed your hatred for another. I'm satisfied and I'm clear that I have expressed my love to another human being completely." We hung up.

From the moment we ended that short conversation, a transformation occurred in Jerry's reality: for the next forty-eight hours there was a flood of telephone calls and personal *messages from people all over the country to thank him and acknowledge him for thoughtful and loving things he had done for them in the past; some were as far back as ten years or more. His patients improved. His office books cleared up. His car ran perfectly. He came across people in the street whom he had not seen for months or years, some of whom fell into his arms, embracing.*

He found he was able to express love and to receive it. When he called me three days after our "hate" conversation, there was a buoyant, alive and vibrant Jerry on the line—one I had never heard before. I wept tears of joy.

He has had some ups and downs since, as is natural when one begins to function from a new space, for the ego does not give up without some skirmishes. In his process since then, many pretenses, beliefs and assumptions have come up for him to take responsibility for. They were, in a sense, buried under his profound unwillingness to give and accept love.

I suggest that before you read the next chapter, you take some time to look at your own reality and discover any insights for yourself. What are your reactions when someone clearly expresses love to you? How do others react when you clearly express love to them? How often have you felt vulnerable? Rejected? Depressed? Anxious? Sad? Annoyed? Angry? Especially with respect to the issue of loving or being loved? What underlies the issue of love in your life?

VI.
A Lesson from Jerry

The first insight that struck me from the interaction with Jerry was this: he did not reject people, he rejected their love. When a woman began to express her love for him, he would attack. She could only experience being rejected and never notice that it was her love that was being rejected. Look and see if this may apply in your life.

When you thought you were rejected by another, could it have been your expression of love that was attacked and rejected rather than you? Or when you have rejected another (lost interest in, and all the other forms of rejection), is it possible that it was his or her love which was threatening to you?

The truth is that love is threatening to the ego, that is, the person you think you are. The person you think you are depends for its existence on not being loved. When we express ourselves as an ego, we receive expression as an ego. If you can see for yourself right now that you were never rejected, only your love was, you may notice a great reduction in guilt and self-invalidation, and a greater experience of self-esteem.

And if you look at the people in your life whom you have rejected, you may find that the trigger was the fear of accepting love with all of its imagined obligations and threats of loss. I say threats of loss, because I have observed many people who withhold loving and being loved because of a shocking loss in the past followed by a decision such as "I'll never love again," or "I'll never be loved again," or, "I'm not loveable"—made in order to avoid another loss. One can only have the illusion of losing that to which one is, in the illusion-reality, attached, which one "needs." For me, attached means simply, "I need you for my survival in a hostile world." Or, "I need you for approval from others, or to prove that I'm OK to myself." And watch out: if you are the one who is needed, you will be the one whose "survival" is threatened next.

So the first thing I became clear about with Jerry is that

people do not reject people, only the ego rejects being loved. The second thing I became clear about was that I had experienced with Jerry what I suspected or knew about all along, and now knew experientially; that only two things are going on in the world, only one of which is real:

Love (emotion and creation), and the barriers to the experience and expression of love.

The third clarity occupies the rest of this book. Suppressed emotion is the major barrier to the experience of love. As soon as Jerry expressed his resentment and hatred of me, and I neither resisted, nor was affected by his expression, and I could understand why he had those emotions, and had the right to express them, a transformation occurred. It was a perfect example of the miracle of true communication, wherein there is the intentional recreation of another's experience. It did not matter that I was the one to whom he expressed his hatred. What mattered was that he did express it to the one at whom it was directed. His natural ability to express and receive love was immediately unblocked.

He had suppressed all feeling and emotion early in his life. Our interaction last summer did not result in the release of all negative and positive emotions: it did reduce his fear of feeling and expressing, so that during the last six months he has been able to allow himself to have and to express anger, rage, grief, and huge waves of fear. He is now much closer to being clear that his feelings and emotions, including love, will not harm himself or others. And he has moved and evolved from being the victim of his reality toward experiencing being the cause of it. He is real.

PAUSE

While writing the last two chapters I noticed something about the form or structure of what I was writing: it corresponds to the classical sonata-allegro form in music — the form of most first movements of symphonies. That is:

1. An introduction which establishes context, or background.

2. The exposition in which two main themes are introduced, with bridging between the two.

3. A repeat of the exposition.

4. A development section, in which the two themes are used as the basis for a free dramatic exploration of pure expression. New thematic material is introduced, or grows out of the two main themes.

5. A recapitulation, a restatement of the two main themes, this time often in the same key.

6. A coda, or conclusion.

The themes are, of course, love and responsibility. We have completed the introduction, exposition, and the repeat exposition, and are now going into the development section.

VII.
The Mechanisms

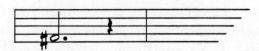

I am going to simplify by condensing the negative emotions into four categories, knowing at the same time, that this is artificial, and that emotions do not exist linearly. They exist outside of time and place. We would have to describe them in our linear and time-oriented language, as existing spirally, blending into each other with infinite gradations of quality and depth. Our labels for them are entirely artificial and synthetic, and need to be transcended. Our labels represent concepts of emotion, not direct experience. For me, experientially, the range from deepest despair to the height of ecstasy actually represents one emotion; and it is that which fuels, provides the energy for, creation. Out of a limitless range of probably creations, what you and I cause to manifest in our independent illusion-realities is a function of the emotional energy giving power to our beliefs and imagination. Charge up your intent with enough fear, and you will create a reality which scares the hell out of you. Charge it with anger and hostility, and you will have an angry and hostile environment. Charge it with joy, celebration, and love, and your illusion-reality will reflect that back to you.

To return to the four categories of "negative emotions," they are:

1. Anger

2. Fear

3. Grief

4. Apathy

Ultimately, we will all have to take responsibility for having created the emotions. For now, let us deal with the effects of our creations. Whatever reality we create (in the illusion), we are the effect of that creation. We created bodies, and immediately became the effect of bodies. We created emotions and became the effect of emotions. That is the way it is, and there is no way out of it.

There are, however, three ways we can hold, or come from, or deal with, being the effect of our creations:

1. Resist being the effect.

     or   Suffering

2. Succumb to being the effect.

3. Accept, take back responsibility for, having created that of which you and I are the effect.

The third option leads to mastery of the illusion-reality. The first two lead to "total determinism"—another way of saying "total victim of everyone and everything in your reality."

One could say that what enlightenment, transformation, and mastery are about is taking back personal responsibility for having caused that of which you are the effect.

So what I want to accomplish in this chapter is to build a structure from which you can see that the third option is available to you. If you do not want to give up suffering and victimhood, stop here. Only your powerful, emotional desire to experience love and responsibility will give your intention the energy for you to climb to the top of this staircase. You can see the view only from the top. And the next stairway does not begin until you have reached the top of this one.

We form our illusion-reality from our thoughts: those thoughts which become beliefs, assumptions, considerations, organizing principles, judgements, and evaluations. I will call beliefs all the kinds of thoughts which we use to structure our realities.

Where do our beliefs come from? They come from decisions we have made about how to survive. We not only make them up ourselves, but we are deluged with beliefs from our parents, from our families, from teachers, friends, what we read, what society believes. Those which fit our unique decisions about making it in the world, we make our own. Those which do not fit, we discard, make wrong, or disbelieve. Beliefs are not good, bad, right, or wrong. They just are. There are beliefs which, when held to be so, limit our potential to expand, to grow, to experience the depth and breadth of our ability to love and be loved. There are other beliefs which are more fun to have, and which we can use as tools, ladders, or stairways to expand and evolve. We cannot get rid of all of our beliefs. We can only take responsibility for them. When we do, the belief loses its command value over us as we shape our individual illusion-realities.

All of our negative beliefs and belief systems can be traced back to the fundamental notion that we cause nothing; that we are ourselves the result of our environments; that we have to dominate, sacrifice, put up with, or succumb to an essentially impersonal, unloving world.

The illustration in Chapter II of physical symptoms clearing up when the underlying belief is discovered are all excellent examples of what happens when one is willing to be responsible for an uncovered belief. Beliefs completely determine your reality when held as the truth.

I referred earlier to the belief I had that I "needed" certain other people to be whole and complete within myself. I did not tell you how I came to recognize that I operated my life out of that belief. Some years ago I went to a day-long course on relationships, and I attended not only as a participant, but also as a physician to be available should any medical emergencies arise from the large group attending the course. I sat where I could be found easily, and also carried a beeper. No medical problems arose for several hours.

Then, just as the course leader said, "What we're going to do next is give you the opportunity to identify the act or system you use which is your barrier to having satisfying relationships, and . . ."

At that moment my beeper sounded. I was needed to see a young woman who was having what is medically known as an anxiety-hyperventilation episode. I saw her, and it took about an hour for her symptoms to subside. And of course, I had missed the opportunity (I thought) to discover my belief system or "act," my barrier to satisfying relationships. The ego's resistance to getting found out is enormous.

Two days later I was reading a book by Jane Roberts in which she mentioned how certain people in the helping or healing professions do it out of a need for recognition and approval, the need to be put on a pedestal, etc., and how that diluted or undermined the value of the help or healing. I suddenly burst into tears. She was describing me. I could see that I had actually created that incident of being needed at the relationships event as a demonstration of my basic belief, and did not see the lesson until two days later.

Why else would I have been a doctor? Why else did I have to manipulate Jamie and Jamie II into needing me? The tears, as my tears usually are, represented a mixture or grief and joy: grief for the waste, blame, the invalidation of myself and others, and joy for the release from that compulsion. Now I could be needed without having to be needed. I could also be unneeded without that being a threat. I immediately observed the shift in my reality; the joy and satisfaction I received from my work and my relationships soared and continue to soar. I do, from time to time, have to have conversations with a young Bobby I have inside (myself as a child) who still thinks and will always think that he has to be put on a pedestal. I simply give him permission to have his own reality, and please do not spill his over into mine.

So, my computation way back and very early in this lifetime was, "I need you, so in order to keep you around, I'll get you to need me."

This brings up a very nasty attribute of that part of us, the ego, for which pure surviving is the major issue. It goes like this:

"In order to survive, I must be separate from you; and I must maintain that separation, especially in a group of more than two persons. If I depend on you too much, or get too attached to you and lose separation, you could hurt me, destroy me, so I must at all costs maintain my separation from you."

Now what do you suppose the ego comes up with as the most efficient way to separate ourselves from almost everyone else? Think about it a moment before you read on.

It is this: if I have an exclusive relationship with one person, that will automatically exclude me and maintain my separation from all others. And as soon as I have that exclusive relationship with one other, I have to start the process of separating from him or her to re-establish separation. Then comes the double bind: I need you for my survival, and with you I may not survive. I cannot live with you and I cannot live without you.

If you have been looking beneath what I have just been saying, you will see that the whole mechanism would have to come from a position of no responsibility, a position called "victim." The important emotion here is fear—fear of merging with another and fear of being separate. It is fear cutting both ways. The emotion most opposite and antagonistic to love is fear.

You may well ask, "Do you mean that people should not have exclusive relationships?" I do not mean that. A relationship based on fear has little room for the experience or expression of love. Only by allowing yourself to be afraid, and taking responsibility for your fear by asking "why am I afraid?", can a relationship based on love, commitment, and trust come about.

I have illustrated several ways so far that you can use to identify and take responsibility for the beliefs which are your barriers to love. Here is another method; if you are upset with something or someone, or having a problem, or something or someone is causing you trouble, then:

1. Tell yourself exactly what happened; who did what, who said what, when, where.

2. Write down the emotions you have related to that incident.

3. Use your intelligence and intuition to see what beliefs could generate those emotions given the circumstances

of what happened (No.1). Write down all the beliefs
you think of which, if you had them, could account for
the emotions you wrote down.

4   When you have exhausted all the beliefs, go back and
read the list, and re-read it.

You will begin to notice that some are specific beliefs, and
some are general. Now see if you can find a single, general belief
which could be the generator of the whole list. When you discover it, you will notice that every moment of your life, including your thoughts, the circumstances, your evaluations and
judgements, even the people in your life, were there because of
that belief. From the central belief, you create both your reality
and your perception of reality.

I recently found what I thought was one of those generator
beliefs, and then discovered a vicious one under it. The one I
found first was "I am unable and insufficient to have a long
term, romantic, physically intimate relationship." A few days
later the more basic statement revealed itself: "I love you, but
you don't love me because you can't!" The pages of my life
flipped through fast when I saw that one generator belief. In
every relationship I had, starting with my friend in the seventh
grade, that had been there. I do not know when I decided "you
don't love me because you can't," and it was obviously one of
the basic generator beliefs of my life.

It is critically important that you locate those few limiting
beliefs which run your life. Each upset you have is another opportunity to use the simple method above to locate and make
conscious your limiting beliefs.

To review briefly: our beliefs come from decisions we made
about surviving. These decisions come from and generate emotions which are suppressed. Out of the beliefs and suppressed
emotions come our thoughts, evaluations, judgements, criti-

cisms, resentments, regrets, and more decisions and beliefs. We take these things as reality, "the way things really are," as if we found them rather than made them up.

Right here, some definite opposition to what I have just said will likely have come up. You may be thinking something like: "Wait a minute! This guy is nuts. My thoughts and beliefs and judgements and evaluations come from what I observe around me, what other people say and do, how people and things behave around me. They come from what I've been taught and learned and noticed and figured out and . . ." and on and on.

Too bad, but that is backward. Your environment is a reflection of your beliefs. Your beliefs come first, then they are materialized in the illusion-reality. You are the source of your beliefs, your environment is not. The only place you can effectively take responsibility for your reality is in looking at, and taking responsibility for, your beliefs. How do you do that? By doing it. Responsibility is a generating context. There is no technique for it. It is a choice you make.

Is there someone you know fairly well who you think of as stupid? If you look closely at your beliefs about that person, especially those you formed when you first met, you will probably notice that the belief came first, then that person appeared stupid and behaved stupidly, and you got to be right. Now if you can get clear with yourself that you made up that belief, this is what taking responsibility looks like. And what will happen next is that that person will no longer appear stupid to you!

Try it. It will give you an experience of who is creating your reality.

The issues of love and responsibility are so entwined that it is impossible to discuss one without the other. The way these things can be separated for a discussion of resolving dissonance to harmony, is this:

The experience of responsibility (cause) is arrived at by dealing with and transcending survival issues.

The experience of love is arrived at through the experience of responsibility, and releasing and allowing a natural flow of all emotion.

There are two survival mechanisms which I have barely touched on so far, but now need to be explored. The two mechanisms are related, in that the first derives from the second. You may find it difficult to keep your attention on what you are about to read. This is not material that the ego, or survival aspect of ourselves wants to hear. That resistance may result in sleepiness or inability to follow what I say. Negative emotions may come up, and you may have physical discomfort to prevent you from understanding these mechanisms.

I.   THE FIRST MECHANISM: Withheld communication

The first mechanism has to do with the damage we do to others and to ourselves. The open kind of damage—violating bodies or things—results from withheld negative emotions which are held back until there is an explosion (damage to another) or an implosion (damage to one's own body, as accidents, illness, arthritis, cancer, etc.)

The hidden kind of damage is far more destructive than physical violence because it damages the self-esteem of both people. It is this hidden withheld damage I will discuss. The downhill course of my relationship with Jamie came not from physical violence, but from the insidious, cruel, covert damage of withholding the desire to harm another, or doing damaging acts and withholding responsibility for them. What is worse, damage is done when you consider it is done. We are speaking here of your reality which is created by your considerations and beliefs.

The result of withholding responsibility for the damage you have done to others is a slow physical paralysis and loss of the ability to act, to function, and to live. I refer here to premature aging. Paralyzing strokes can be the result—and finally, death. It is as though our natural integrity—our higher selves, if you will—stop us from doing more damage, and the destruction is turned on ourselves. The world's great tragedies, especially those of Shakespeare, brilliantly demonstrate this principle. All lies are examples of this kind of damage.

It starts like this: suppose you steal fifty cents from your mother's purse and do not tell her. You have just cut off an area of communication with her and others and you are afraid of her now, and afraid to tell her so. You can no longer discuss money with her, or stealing, or lying, or purses, without having your attention and emotions drawn to that incident. You are afraid of being found out. You notice, however, that God did not strike you with lightning, in fact, you were not even punished and this gives you permission to do it again—maybe steal a dollar next time. Because of increasing fear of punishment it becomes harder and harder to tell your mother what you did, and your life begins to be about the fear of being discovered. What you do not notice is that you have started a process of self punishment far more severe than that which would happen by telling the truth. Because nobody else is punishing you, you again give yourself permission to go on stealing. If you set it up to get caught, and you tell all the truth, that is the end of it. If you do not get caught, and you continue to withhold the truth, you will eventually end up having severe problems with money, especially with people stealing from you.

In consulting people with money problems, I have frequently discovered such a simple, seemingly harmless, early experience. Once the truth is told, problems with money clear up fast.

It should be obvious, in this simple example, that if you were the child who stole the money, and never told, the flow of love for your mother would be cut off and replaced by fear. Mother now becomes a threat because she might find out. You begin to act defensive around her, and she would not know what the problem was.

I consider that the example I have just given should resonate with your own experience, and that it is not too difficult to understand. The really tough example, the one most of us do not want to confront, is that the most vicious damage is done by believing our negative thoughts about others, or ourselves, and then withholding them. In a later chapter we will look at that kind of damage.

We could categorize nearly all of these damaging thoughts under the headings of judgements and evaluations. These go in two directions: outward to others, inward to oneself, or both. The most powerful example of a judgement of another is resentment. Regret is the inward form.

The definition of resentment I prefer is this: a feeling of bitter hurt or indignation, from a sense of being injured or offended. One could as well say "a judgement of having been hurt." I am not going to list examples of resentments; they are too common. You know one when you have one or see one. And you know how you treat people whom you resent for something they did to you; the range of your reactions varies from suspicion to viciousness, from defensiveness or revenge to exclusion of that person from your life. Love does not have a chance.

There is not the slightest chance that we can fully love anyone if we carry around even a single resentment toward just one person. That is a strong statement, and I mean it. Why do I say that? Because that one resentment signifies that you have not really experienced being the cause of your life; you have not looked at the resentment or that person from the position of responsibility, nor have you released the anger which you are so jealously hanging onto. You see, we do have a moment of choice in how we react to others, and how we interpret their actions. If you consider (believe) that what another did or said damaged you, then there is an automatic reaction waiting for you. It comes from your store of ego tricks for surviving. But there is a moment of choice, a moment when you can choose not to react as though you were damaged. I did not say you could pretend not to be damaged; that is just another survival reaction. You are running your show; you are writing your script. If you are writing a war story, then you will have to stick to and hang on to resentments and defensive / offensive actions and their inevitable result: suffering. And there is nothing wrong with that. Just do not waste any time or fret or wonder why you do not have love, peace, or happiness in your life. Those are not available to you.

If you have had enough of suffering, then here is what to do about resentments in two words: communicate them. Tell the person you resent exactly what it is you resent, when it happened, all the details. Well, you may ask, if it is that easy, how come I have not done that before? You can probably answer that question before I do. It is fear that stops you. It was fear that stopped you from telling your mother you took some money from her purse; from telling your husband or wife that you wanted to, or did, screw somebody else; from telling someone you lied to them. And on and on. You withheld these things because you were afraid. Afraid of what? Punishment? Retribution? Losing someone? Being sent away from your family? What if it got in the newspaper? What if people really knew how bad I am? Well the truth is, all those people are so busy making sure you do not find out about them that they do not really care about what you have done or have not done.

What are the real payoffs for hanging onto your resentments? They are hanging onto your judgements and punishing thoughts or acts; clinging to avoidance of impact; storing your anger; feeding self-importance and self-pity; and not last or least, the avoidance of responsibility: avoiding being willing to experience being the cause of your life. So long as you can blame someone else for your suffering and for being unloved, etc. you do not have to be responsible.

Suppose the person you resent is dead or not available? Tell yourself what happened, then imagine telling that person the whole truth about your resentment. You will notice an interesting result. If you tell the resentment to the person you resent in the form of an attack, to reinforce what a terrible person he or she is, it obviously will not work. You will still be playing war games. Hold off until you know that you are the source of your reaction to the other person. Here is the real source of the resentment mechanism: nobody ever ever "damaged" you unless you had damaged that person first, in thought or deed, or both.

Some years ago I was consulting a woman, a housewife and mother, who said, "You know, it really annoys me when my husband sits at the dinner table and doesn't use his napkin!"

There was a pause, during which the following mechanism flashed through me: if she was creating her own reality, why would she have her husband do something that annoyed or upset her? Answer: her annoyance must justify something that she had done to him and was withholding. If she had even had a damaging thought—a thought about damaging him—and never told him, she would have to have him behave in a way which would justify, or make her right about having such a thought. And she would actually look for such justifications in his behavior and find them.

I told her what I had just seen, and we started looking at what she had thought about him, or done to him, and never told him. In only a few minutes we got to the original one, the fearful thought that she had had, and which had persisted since he had asked her to marry him. It was: "I'm afraid that I will kill you," and "I want to kill you."

That thought came from the bad, evil, terrible person who she thought she really was, and who had to be hidden from herself as much as possible, and certainly hidden from others. Her presentation, or act, was the complete opposite of that terrible person: kind, considerate, loving, etc. The trouble was, she knew it was a pretense to keep anyone from finding out how bad she really was. She could not tell her husband that thought because it would reveal that ugly self she thought she really was. Who could love or marry or even want to be with such a bad person?

In the remainder of the session, she came to see that she was neither that no-good person nor the pretense of goodness; she was that which had made up both. Who she really was contained both, and she could now tell her husband her horrible, *fearful thought, and she did. Their relationship soared to places they had only dreamed of before.*

II.   THE SECOND MECHANISM: Being "good" or "bad"

The ego, or that part of the mind which considers itself vulnerable and must survive at all costs, put this one together very early in its development, and holds onto it ever so dearly and tenaciously.

Remember, in this illusion-reality, nothing exists without its opposite. One could say that the chief survival function of the ego is to make value judgements about each pair of opposite qualities that it encounters. The judgements are made on the basis of what has seemed to work to guarantee its own survival. We have evaluations and judgements about good/bad, right/wrong, responsibility/irresponsibility, kindness/cruelty, loyalty/disloyalty, and all other pairs of opposites of which you and I can think.

The force or fuel which drives the ego is a fantasy it has made up about how life should look if the ego were eternal. What or how you would be, what you would be doing or not doing, what you would have or not have. This is the place where we live happily ever after, the place where fairy-tales end, the place in the movies where the credits roll. You know—peace and love and cottages and loving children and lots of money and lots of comfort and no problems . . . few notice that there would be eternal stagnation, no growth, so boring that you would gladly go back to the world as you knew it. But, that is what ultimate survival looks like to the ego, an attempt to make a heaven on earth, frozen in time, with no change, no stress, no challenge, and it always exists in the future—this is never it!

How do we, as ego, try to get there? First, we decide on a way of presenting ourselves to our parents which will get us what we need to survive: fed, clothed, attention, touched, and so forth. Suppose we decide on being the kind of person who would present these qualities:

friendly
loving
trustworthy
honest
industrious
responsible
happy
attractive.

And then try them out. It seems to work! But suppose a
brother or sister comes along, or a cousin, or friend, who is also
exhibiting those qualities to your parents. What if your parents
find the other person to be more friendly, more trustworthy,
etc., than you? Suddenly you are in competition with everybody who is exhibiting those qualities. You have to be more
friendly and loving, more honest and trustworthy, etc. than just
about everybody else, or your security is threatened. Also, as
you grow older, the fantasy described above begins to build up.

Over time it begins to be obvious that no matter how
attractive you are, how responsible you are, how honest you
are, you are not getting what you really want, that is, safety
now, and ultimate safety from threat and attack in the fantasy
scenario of the future.

Some major shocking event happens which proves to you
the futility of ever getting what you want, so you make a
decision. The decision is to reverse all of those great qualities
you originally decided on, since they are not working. So you
become:

unfriendly
unloving
untrustworthy
dishonest

lazy
irresponsible
unhappy, depressed
ugly, unattractive.

Maybe that will work. Over time, it seems to produce results at first, but again, you finally decide you are getting further away from your goal of "happy every after," and during or
after another shocker that really jars you, you decide to change.
In case you have not noticed, I am describing the mechanism of
conversion, the "conversion experience." Change to what?
Well, maybe those qualities we tried before will work this time,
or we forget that they did not work before.

I am not suggesting that all these qualities shift from positive to negative or negative to positive at once. But in general
there is a cluster which shifts, or one or more pairs may be given
up altogether.

This mechanism results in the belief that there is a person
you really are, that you are afraid you are, that has to be hidden, and another person you present to the world. If you are
running mostly the "positive" qualities for show, then the person you are afraid you are is the one with the opposite, negative
qualities. If you are presenting the negative side, then the person
you are afraid you really are is the good, honest, responsible
one.

It is easy to test the validity of all this yourself, and here are
the tests:

1. If you look around at the people you are most comfortable with, you will notice that the qualities of their presentation are similar to yours—not exactly, but close. The
problem here is that you compete with others with respect

to those qualities. If you are not more honest, or more responsible, or more whatever, you feel threatened, and will often have damaging thoughts or actually do unethical damage to those with whom you are competing. It often occurs with your best friends. You can supply your own examples here.

This is one origin of the first mechanism.

2. Now look at the kinds of people you do not like to be around, feel uncomfortable with, would not be caught dead with. What qualities do they have which you find irritating or which you actually abhor? If you do this honestly, you will see that the qualities these people present to the world (in your illusion-reality) are the very ones you are hiding from yourself and others; they represent the person you are afraid you are.

The only reason you could make those qualities wrong in others is that you have made them wrong in yourself.

This is the major source of the damage we do to others and ourselves, by our thoughts or by our deeds, or both.

I have purposely left the major dipolar opposite to point out now. It is male/female. It is such a powerful and deeply routed symbol of that Prime Condition for the existence of the illusion-reality, that we have mostly forgotten that it is nothing more than a symbol. The Prime Condition is positive/negative: the nature of vibration. That which vibrates, waves, must have a movement in one direction (positive) followed by a point of zero movement, then movement in the opposite direction (negative). Movement in one direction only obviously produces no vibration. The essence and nature of the illusion-reality is vibra-

tion. It is vibration. All dichotomies or dipolar opposites that
we know are simply symbols for that which is necessary for the
existence of all things in heaven and earth: vibration. No vibration; no mass, no energy, no thing. The essence of life is to and
fro, back and forth, in and out—alternating opposites—vibra-
tions.

When we judge and evaluate that it is better to be positive
than negative or better to be negative than positive, better to be
a man than a woman, or better to be a woman than a man (and
that is what we are doing with all dichotomies; all dipolar opposites), we are lying about the very essence of our existence, and
suffer the consequences of lies: suffering and effort.

A very close friend and mentor of mine said that if you are
concerned or having problems with masculinity or femininity,
whether what you are doing or thinking is masculine of feminine, you look down between your legs and resolve your con-
cern. If you look down there and see a penis, then what you are
doing is masculine, whether it is needlepoint or digging ditches.
If you look down there and see a vagina, then what you are
doing is feminine, whether it is needlepoint or digging ditches.

That ends the discussion on masculine or feminine. As
usual, the truth is disarmingly simple.

What I have described in discussing this mechanism could be called the Wheel of Life. We persist in trying a group of qualities or their opposites to get to the happy-ever-after place, over and over, and over . . . sometimes switching (converting) several times in a lifetime, sometimes spending an entire lifetime in one mode or the other.

What is worse, Genesis 1:27 says: "So God created man in his own image. . . ." We create our illusion-reality people to conform to our own images of ourselves (do you know any people who are not, anatomically, male or female?), so that just about everybody you know looks like either the person you are pretending to be or the person you are afraid you are.

But not quite. There is always someone around in your reality who represents who you really are, an embodiment of your positionless Being or Self, and therein lies the secret of getting off the endless wheel. A relationship with this person can be transforming.

The risk I have taken in going into some deatil about these ego mechanisms is that you will believe that they are real. You already do believe that they are real, or they would not be so prevalent. If you and I stopped believing in them they would disappear. My purpose in describing them is to simply point them out as belief systems which act as barriers to the experience of love. You cannot take responsibility for a belief unless you know what the belief is. There is no such thing as "a person you are afraid you are" except in your imagination. You made that person up and you can unmake him or her any time you want. It is like a child who draws a picture of a terrible monster with fangs and red eyes and breathing fire, and then is frightened. You can give up such childish games.

Now we will go back to where we started this development section, and look at emotions.

If our emotions are influenced by beliefs, then it would seem that if we could take responsibility for our beliefs, our emotions and our illusion-reality would transform. Actually, you would transform. The illusion does not transform; it just changes or disappears. That is the same as saying that you cannot transform a belief, but you open the door to your transformation by acknowledging yourself as the source of beliefs.

From very early in each of our lifetimes, we have been carefully taught, in part by our parents who were similarly taught, and for sure by society, that there is something wrong with having and expressing emotions—positive or negative. Exuberant joy is squelched, along with anger, fear and grief. Even apathy is made wrong or worse, right. We learned that people (including ourselves) get their "feelings hurt." We learned how to avoid hurting another's feelings in order to manipulate and get what we want. Women particularly are put down as not being lady-like if they express anything more than tears. Men, in our society, are given more latitude to express anger, for example, but not grief or fear. That would not be manly. Sometimes it is OK for parents to raise emotional hell with each other, but children are not allowed to do the same. So a lot of children decide that they will never get angry or behave as their parents behave.

Why do we set up realities in which emotions are suppressed, and provide ourselves with belief systems which justify that suppression?

Emotions and their expressions do not damage people. They do not damage the person who has the emotion nor is the recipient damaged. The suppression of emotion is damaging to both. Why? Because what damages people is dishonesty. Emotion does not damage people, dishonesty (withheld emotion) does damage people.

If you are joyous and pretend you are not, you damage yourself and others. If you are angry, or afraid, or sad, or apathetic, and pretend you are not, even to yourself, you damage yourself and others. When you are hiding or suppressing any emotion, you seem unreal to others. Others cannot communicate with you and you cannot communicate with others. There is absolutely no space for love to be experienced or shared —you are too busy pretending.

You can begin now by noticing when you suppress or pretend about emotions. Review the day you read this or the day before and notice how many times you denied an emotion its expression. Then notice how you justified doing that: how you always justify it. Justifications are necessary only for lies. The truth about your feelings needs no justification. Your feelings and emotions are, they exist like trees and birds and people and storms exist. They are not lies. You are the only liar when you deny or suppress your feelings.

If you will openly and honestly allow yourself to have, own and express any and all emotion, you would discover that upward spiral: grief would dissolve into anger which would dissolve into—at the top of the spiral—love. And the more depth you allow yourself in the experience of all the emotions, the more deeply will you allow yourself to experience love. The range of emotions is not from negative to positive, but rather from intense to non-intense, real to suppressed. What is important, therefore, is your willingness to experience the intensity of emotions—the willingness to experience the intensity of love as well as the intensity of no love.

You may have already observed that we are discussing the "threshing-floor:"

". . . But if in your fear you would seek only love's peace

and love's pleasure,

    Then it is better for you that you cover your naked-
ness and pass out of love's threshing-floor,

    Into the seasonless world where you shall laugh, but
not all of your laughter, and weep, but not all of your tears
. . ."

                    THE PROPHET
                    Kahlil Gibran

    A word of caution here. I am not and will not advocate
physical violence. Violence is born out of the suppression of
emotion, not out of its release.

    Nature's violence—floods, earthquakes, hurricanes, dam-
aging storms—are bred from and out of massed suppressed
human emotion in the areas the disasters occur. This is not so
far-fetched if you realize that each of us creates his or her reality,
individually and en masse, and the "natural" phenomena are
simply macrocosmic representations of what is going on with
each of us, individually.

I had my first direct experience of who is running the weather on that Memorial Day weekend boat trip.

When we made rendezvous with the houseboats, it was sprinkling and the sun was behind a large dark cloud. I went below, closed my eyes, imagined a large hole appearing through the clouds, letting the sun through, and said: "We will have sunshine wherever we are for the next two days."

At that moment my guests shouted, "Hey Bob! Come on up—the sun is shining."

And for the next two days, although it was generally cloudy and rainy, we had sunshine through a hole in the clouds. Believable? No. Did it really happen? Yes. And many times thereafter.

War obviously represents the violent release of suppressed emotion. No particular war will establish the end of wars, make the world safe for anything or ensure the loving brother/sisterhood of the human race. Peace and a cooperating world community will occur only when each of us, individually creates realities of peace and loving cooperation in our immediate environments. The celebration of our love and commitment to each other locally will generate the energy required to establish an active and productive peace to the four corners of this earth.

Until you and I regain our ability to experience and express love, the rest of the people of the planet will be in a state of unrest.

It appears that the basic negative emotion is fear. We do not express our other emotions because we are afraid to express them. Least of all do we express fear, for that would seem to render us vulnerable, weak, subject to attack and annihilation. And we are afraid to experience loving and being loved for the same reasons!

Probably, by now, you have asked yourself: "If I create my own reality, why can't I have it the way I want it?"

The primary cause is fear. To test this out, think of something you really want that you do not have, and then list ten reasons why you are afraid to have it. Usually the one or two fears that are keeping you from having it will appear on that list, and they will not be the first two or three of which you think. It is scary to find out that you are running your show.

How do you start taking the lid off? You just start—slowly and easily at first. There is no short cut, nor can you put it off, if you want to evolve. The major decision is to stop being dishonest and to stop withholding the expression of your experience. Stop pretending you are what you are not, and are not what you are. If you are annoyed, be annoyed and say so. If you are pleased, be pleased and express it. If you are anxious, terrified, in despair, enraged, let yourself be that. Its expression will harm no one. Its suppression harms everyone.

Seemingly ridiculous little things like saying hello first, remembering to thank someone for something, acknowledging someone for a well-done job will begin to loosen up your self-expression and allow the more fearful emotions to be experienced and expressed more freely. You do not have to believe any of this, nor agree or disagree with it. Try it. See how it works, and be honest with yourself. Your experience is all that is real. And please, no sympathy for yourself or others. That is not an emotion. Sympathy, like guilt, is a synthetic damaging product of our illusion-reality. Sympathy and guilt degrade and damage self-esteem and self-love. Most of us have wanted or given sympathy, thinking it to be synonymous with love. It is not. Nor is guilt an emotion. It is not the result of doing something your conscience tells you you should not have. That is your natural integrity revealing itself. If you look closely at what you feel guilty about, you will find suppressed anger and outrage, which you feel you have no right to express. Trying to make another feel guilty is the same. It is a dishonest ploy to avoid releasing your suppressed anger, hate, or resentment. If someone tells you with emotion that he/she hates you, rejoice, for momentarily it will turn into love. If someone is, or has been trying to make you feel guilty, run away fast for you are about to become the victim of a victim.

I re-emphasize that the expression of emotion is not damaging to anyone. Assertive, yes. Honest, yes. Damaging, no. Expressed emotions do not kill. Suppressed emotions do. If you cower before another's anger, it is only because you are afraid to express your own. Many use their suppressed emotions, especially anger, as a manipulating weapon: "I'm doing you a favor by not letting you know how angry I am." Or, "I won't let him/her know the depth of my love by expressing my grief."

Violence in any form is the result of the sudden release of a massive buildup of suppressed emotion. The fear of violence may be one of our chief justifications for suppression of anger; but that very suppression, built-up over time, is guaranteed to produce violence.

Our emotions or experience, being a part of the real reality, as is love, go with us between lives and continue into other expanded states of spiritual evolvement long after we choose not to return to this physical illusion-reality in bodies. Our "higher" selves will give us unlimited time to learn to own and express our negative and positive emotions. When you choose to evolve, to become self-expressive, is up to you.

The origin of many of our most debilitating and lethal disease states, including cancer, is the result of having suppressed emotions, and then literally giving up hope of ever expressing them. This is the state of apathy and resignation. Sure, you will have the opportunity to start over, and over, and over, until you take responsibility for honestly expressing yourself emotionally. Apathy and depression are dangerous places to be unless you have chosen death as the way out. And it is only a temporary way out, since you will come back for enough lifetimes to handle the emotions in physical life.

If you are noticing some confusion with respect to the separate issues of responsibility and expressing emotions, there is good reason. There is a paradox. It is this: yes, we create our individual realities one-hundred percent. You are alone in it, and everyone and everything else in it is a figment of your imagination. And that is the one statement in this book which is not a belief. It is so. Well, then, if that is so, why would I worry about expressing or suppressing emotions? If you are only a figment of my imagination, then I should be able to treat you any way I damn well please.

But here is the paradox: we also created the reality of having impact—emotional impact—on each other. And why did we do that? To learn the lesson of responsibility, to rediscover our ability to respond, and to take back personal responsibility for our unique and separate realities. If we deny our emotional impact on others, we are stuck in victimhood. If we deny others' impact on ourselves, we are stuck in victimhood. We built in the vulnerability—the capacity to hurt and be hurt—in order to lead ourselves toward responsibility and freedom. Why are we here? Why are we in physical form? To explore the arena of emotion; to learn to have fun being physical, and to be successful at creating our reality, with love.

Down at the bottom of, covered up by, hidden by these massive suppressed emotions, is a gift. The next chapter is about that gift.

VIII.
Love and Responsibility

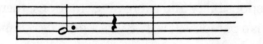

A gift which enables us to take back our personal power is precious beyond money and wealth. A victim is one who has given away responsibility to circumstances, then blames circumstances for having power over him or her.

Our word creates our illusion-realities—our word fueled by emotion. The trouble is, we not only forget what our "word" was, we forget that our reality was literally spoken into existence by what we said.

So buried at the bottom of a deep sea of suppressed emotion, lies our forgotten word—the statement we made which became law, the organizing principle, of our individual lives and our perception of the universe. Once you have recognized one of these statements, you will see how it works. Recognition of one of these statements will open a door for you to locate other statements. The key to this recognition is your willingness and desire to acknowledge being the source of the statement you made, which is easy, once you become aware of the "buried" statement.

Last summer, at the end of a weekend course I was leading, a very perceptive woman participant told me privately that several times during the weekend she noticed a look of sadness about my face, and directly experienced that emotion, apparently coming from me.

I said, "I wasn't aware of that; thanks for telling me. I'll check it out."

As I drove home I did notice a lump in my throat, and decided that if there were suppressed grief there, I would let it come up. By the time I got home tears had started. I thought it would not hurt to have some reinforcement, so I put on the first movement of the Tchaikowsky 6th Symphony. By the climax of that movement, I was massively sobbing—louder than the music. I was at all times aware of expressing the grief, could have stopped it, always opted to let it play out.

After fifteen minutes, the grief and sobbing began to subside and suddenly I became conscious of the words: "Daddy . . . please . . . love . . . me!"

Within the next minute, the following insight became crystal clear: first, "Daddy please love me!" was a request I had never made to him. I had never asked him that. I withheld it. Beneath that I saw that I was the one who had decided that he did not love me. It had nothing to do with him. And underneath that I saw what had happened.

My father was a large, physically powerful man, with large strong hands. As an infant I looked very fragile to him, and he was afraid he would hurt me accidentally with his strength. I interpreted his hesitance to touch me as, "He doesn't love me," and that interpretation became a decision which became an organizing principle for my life up to that moment last summer.

Of course he loved me; that is why he was afraid of hurting me.

I was attending a six-week summer session between the

freshman and sophomore years in medical school when I met Jamie. I planned to go home to Kansas for the end of the summer, and we would start living together when I returned. My Dad, who was an automobile dealer, had an opportunity to drive a new car to an old friend of ours in Seattle, so we timed my leaving San Francisco with his trip, and I drove to Seattle to meet him, then the two of us drove to the small town in Kansas where I had grown up. I was not completely happy about this because it meant I had to leave Jamie sooner than I wanted. We had not known each other very long, and I was in love.

Instead of the leisurely trip Dad had suggested I take driving up the coast, I waited until the last minute and drove straight through, non-stop, to Seattle, and even so I was about eight hours later than the time we had agreed on to meet. I thought I could not tell Dad the truth about why I was late and why I had driven non-stop, but whatever reason I gave him, he knew it was a lie. He could smell lies coming before they were out of peoples' mouths, and he was always accurate.

On the trip to Kansas I told him about Jamie, and that we were moving in together, to save money, in an apartment which was near the University of California Medical School which belonged to the mother of the mutual friend who had introduced us to each other. Dad did not say much or ask much.

The night we got home, after going to bed, I could hear Dad talking to Mother in another room. I heard every word he said. It was something like: "I'm damned if I can understand why Bob would be moving in with some geezer he doesn't know and who isn't even a medical student . . . watch what I tell ya . . . that guy is either a drunk or after Bob's money, or both."

I could not hear Mom's reply, and then I would hear him take off again in the same vein. At first I panicked, felt guilty, sick at my stomach, and then knew what I had to do. I had to get up when he got up at 5:30 a.m. and tell him the truth.

I do not recall sleeping much after that. Finally I heard him get up and go downstairs to the bathroom, and I got up and said to him through the bathroom door, "Dad, I have something to talk to you about when you're through."

I was shaking with both fright and indignation. He opened the door at once, and I said haltingly, "I heard you and Mom talking last night . . . I heard every word you said. Jamie is OK. He's not a drunk. He has a good job. And . . . I love him."

I had never before seen the change that occurred in his face. The worry and anger disappeared, his face became soft, his blue eyes had tears in them and were loving, and he said, "Bobby, I was just concerned because I love you. I trust you, and I'm sorry."

I burst into tears and fell in his arms.

It was not until last summer, after all that grief discharge that I was able to experience the depth of compassion and love that he had for me, and that was expressed that summer morning in Kansas many years ago. Why so long? Because it was in opposition to the belief which I had made up that he did not love me.

The grief had been built up, so to speak, out of my decision that I was unloved. The intensity and depth of that grief was so great to me as an infant, and so threatening, that I chose to suppress it. And the lid I put on the grief also contained my "word," my statement, my decision, "He doesn't love me."

In Chapter II, I wrote "The state of being which allows us to see that cause is not outside the Self, some call transformation." I experienced transformation. It was not a change in attitude, or point of view or position. It was a true contextual shift from "blaming" my father to one of taking full responsiblity for my experience of him. Transformation requires and asks for no proof. Proof does exist, however. After that day I saw every person in my reality in a different way. I saw and experienced their love for me which had always been there, and to which I had been more or less blind. Once again I saw the intimate connectedness between the experiences of love and responsibility.

The greatest responsibility is required not in giving love, but in receiving it. I used the example of Jerry in Chapter V to point that out. If I can receive 90% of your love and you give 100% of yours, you will get back 90% from me and give me back only 90% of yours. I receive only 81% of that (since that is 90% of 90%) and so on, until the exchange of love spirals rapidly down to zero and on into negative—the "negative" emotions.

To receive love one must first have 100% self-love, self-esteem, trust, and not test the others' love, and be able to return 100%. All beliefs about not being loved and unworthiness and not deserving it must be cleaned out.

IX.
Don't Think 'Positively,' Simply Tell the Truth

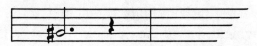

In Chapter VII, we looked at taking responsibility for one's thoughts—for one's beliefs. That means simply acknowledging that you are the source of your thoughts, not your environment, that your environment is a reflection of your thoughts—all of it.

Changing your thoughts does not work. Changing from negative to positive thoughts about yourself or others does not work. What works is being willing to notice that you are the source of your negative thoughts. You do not then have to substitute good thoughts for bad thoughts. When you try to change your negative thoughts without taking responsibility for them, they become more powerful since you are resisting them. That which is resisted or succumbed to becomes manifest in your reality because that which is resisted becomes more real than your pretense. You know you are pretending the positive thoughts, and you know that pretending is dishonest.

When you take responsibility for your thoughts, the love that was always there is revealed.

It is easy to demonstrate the effect your nasty thoughts have on others. I will describe an exercise I have done with individuals and groups which provides the immediate experience of the power of our thoughts:

Two people sit facing each other. They decide who will be the sender and who will be the receiver.

The receiver closes his/her eyes so as not to be influenced by the sender's facial or body expression.

The sender says "Start," and starts thinking nasty, bad, spiteful thoughts about the receiver. The receiver signals when the sender stops thinking the negative thoughts.

The receiver then opens eyes, and they discuss how close the receiver came to knowing when the negative thoughts

stopped. In other words, did the hand signal from the receiver actually coincide with the moment the sender
stopped the negative thoughts.

After three or four runs, the people who are paired change
roles, so that each person gets to send and receive.

The accuracy of the timing has so far been ninety percent
on a first run with groups of people, sitting in pairs, and im-
proves with a few more runs of the exercise.

The usual reaction of the receiver to the negative thoughts
is some uncomfortable or unpleasant body sensation and/or
negative emotion. When the sender has truly let go of (stopped)
the negative thoughts, there is an immediate release in the
receiver of the unpleasant body sensation or emotion.

This exercise is elegant in its simplicity and effectiveness.
Several things become clear:

1.   Our negative thoughts about another have immediate
impact, which stops when the thoughts stop. It is easy to
see why you are physically uncomfortable around some
people, or others are uncomfortable around you. It is also
easy to see why you are uncomfortable, even ill, with
yourself. Your own invalidating thoughts about yourself
have impact on your body.

2.   People doing this exercise have the experience of starting (causing) and stopping (causing) their negative
thoughts about others. Never again can they honestly deny
responsibility for their thoughts and the effects of their
thoughts.

3.   A few people will experience the co-creation of the
exercise; that is, the receiver may notice that he/she is also
causing the start time and stop time: a clear demonstration

of who is responsible for whose illusion-reality!

So far, I have observed that receivers who are not aware of the impact of negative thoughts fall into two extremes. One is the receiver whose experience of love is so clear that there is a kind of immunity from the effects. The other extreme represents people who have been so bombarded with their own or others' negative thoughts about themselves that they have constructed a defensive wall or shield about themselves. In the exercise, it is very easy to see who falls into one or the other mode of experience.

Please be absolutely clear that I am not advocating anything like positive thinking. It does not work. If you are not clear on that, please re-read the first part of this chapter, up to the description of the exercise.

The most effective and efficient way to disappear your negative thoughts is to communicate them. If you communicate them with the intention of hurting another, then you need to say that also. The point is, do not lie, not because it is wrong, but because it does not work. Lying perpetuates the emotion or experience which is lied about.

Only dishonesty does damage, the truth never damages. Remember that fear is an emotion which needs to be fully experienced and expressed. If you are afraid to communicate, you have just sold yourself out to that pale and seasonless existence of never laughing all your laughter, of never weeping all your tears.

And love will be a concept, not a reality.

X.
God or Man?

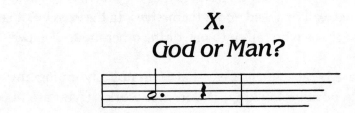

Now for a pulling together of much of the apparently disconnected areas discussed so far. Why have we generally made a mess of love? Why the barriers and blockages? Remember, I cannot tell you the truth about the answers to those questions. I can share with you what I see as true for me, and that may spark your intention to discover your truth.

So: in this chapter I am going to describe two scenarios, neither of which may have anything to do with the truth—and these two scenarios are intimately related.

SCENARIO NUMBER ONE

We enter this physical reality in a tiny, helpless body—a vehicle that cannot walk or talk or crawl or go to the bathroom or get a glass of milk out of the refrigerator. We can cry, suck, and wiggle, and mess up our diapers, and sleep a lot, and that is about it. We do come in "trailing clouds of glory . . . from God, who is our home." (Wordsworth) But it seems we remember that only when we are asleep, and that memory is worthless to get us fed, kept warm, noticed, touched, loved, and diapered. Worse, we are being taken care of by giants on whom we depend completely, and for all we know, they might forget that we are here. We have not decided whether we are loved or not, and we are often fairly sure that we are not even wanted.

And birth itself: "Ye Gods! Squeezing my head through that hole that is too small—being pushed out, ready or not!! Never again!! Jesus! Whatta headache! HELP . . ."

After a missed feeding or two, or being dropped, or stuck with a pin, or cold and wet, or worse, Dad was out drunk when you arrived, or you are given away for adoption—the love issue is settled: "I am NOT loved." That does it.

As that realization slowly dawns, terror sets in: "How can I survive in a world of giants who do not love me? The terror is so great I have to go back to where I came from, or push this apparent reality down and pretend it is not here. And it is the same with the despair, grief, and outrage at having gotten into this lousy problem. When I cry, they think I am hungry or some damned thing; when I am enraged they tell me to shut up!"

So, on top of "I am not loved," the emotions are suppressed very early. And an even more horrible thought sneaks in now and then: "Maybe I am not loveable . . . there may be something wrong with me." Sometimes, oftentimes, that thought takes over and runs your life.

So, here we are, certain that we are not loved, all those overwhelming emotions suppressed, now how are we going to survive? Here is where we start the big pretense: how do I have to be—what do I have to do to get what I must have in order to survive in this hostile world?

Thus your "act" or personality is born. It is your collection of techniques to dominate and manipulate others and to avoid being dominated and manipulated by them. Do I have to be cute? Or yell a lot? Or be mentally deficient? Or sick? Or obnoxious? Or sweet? Whatever works to get attention, sympathy, food, clothing, and pottied. And whatever seemed to work is then indelibly imprinted for future reference. Each one of us comes fully equipped with memories of the lifetimes we survived similar threatening circumstances. So that most of the technique, act, or personality we use to survive is not a matter of conscious choice, as it might seem, but is automatic and unconscious.

So we resist not being loved, and decide, "I won't love you either!," or succumb by trying to love parents or other people who do not love back. So life starts with the establishment of being a victim, a manipulating personality.

To sum up this scenario, it looks like this:

a: I decide I am not loved and probably not loveable.

b: Emotions are suppressed.

c: The survival issues come into play.

Our word, "I am not loved," becomes the organizing principle for the rest of our lives. We create that illusion-reality. The rest of life becomes struggle, effort, suffering, with brief moments of respite.

The only "happiness" we have is a kind of glee at seeing that somebody else has it worse than we have it. Finally, the only ones who feel sorry for us is . . . us.

And love? Forget it.

SCENARIO NUMBER TWO

Once upon a time (and what that really means is that whatever has happened is still happening and always will since all
time is simultaneous) there were—are—in this scenario all
tenses except present tense are meaningless, so I will use conven-
tional tenses, knowing that the past and future exist all at once.
To start again:

Once upon a time there were a group of gods (more accurately, in our terms, "higher consciousness," but let us use "gods"
for short) absolutely loving and endlessly creative. As gods do,
they communicated fully and instantaneously, about their creative experiences. This particular group, simultaneously, saw
that their creations, and other gods' creations, were limited to
gods who knew they were gods. They realized that there was a
whole tremendous area of potential experience which gods had
not yet experienced directly. They had a conversation that went
something like:

"What would happen if we made up a universe, or a bunch
of universes, in which a part of each of us will forget that we are
gods. We would then have experiences that we could not have
while knowing that we are gods. And we will fix it up so that
eventually (time was born with that word) we will remember,
since we do not want to be stuck in that or any creation forever.

"Now let us see—what qualities would we have to pretend
not to have if we are going to experience being ungodlike? We
cannot give up being eternal and infinite and having free will,
obviously. But we could pretend that we could cease existing,
and be finite and limited. It looks like we could solve the whole
thing by pretending that we do not love absolutely and unconditionally; and pretend that we do not create things instantaneously. In other words, pretend that we are not the cause of

anything. We could make things like houses and babies and cars and paintings and say that that is what creating is. Oh yeah — we could do that if we said that what is illusion is actually solid and that what is real is an illusion. That would be terrific!!"

Then one god said, representing the many, "I know what we could do: let us invent something called process; it will have seven steps, and everything in this new universe will move through seven steps; we will have to invent time, and the process will work like this. All beginnings will be the first step, and that will represent freedom with no responsibility. Then, everything that begins will be drawn toward the fourth step, losing freedom all the while, until freedom seems to be lost at the fourth level: total determinism, or no freedom, no responsibility. And here is where choice and free will come in: if someone chooses to take responsibility in step four, that person or thing will then be in step five, and moving toward step seven, which is total freedom with total responsibility."

Another god continued, "Yeah! That sounds terrific! And how about this: up through level four, it looks like all there is is surviving. But in level four, if one of our parts we send down there says, 'there must be more to life than surviving,' we'll help him or her to remember that he or she does have free will and choice."

A third said, "And let's have the whole thing be an arena to explore emotions, and through that, people will have the opportunity to transform all emotions into love!"

And a fourth god said, "Yes! And whoever really discovers how to have fun and to be successful in creating his or her reality, with harm to none, and who loves himself or herself unconditionally, that person will have graduated from the physical universe. And we will welcome him or her back home if he or she so chooses."

And so it was—is—and shall be.

Of course, any god could enter into the physical system to try out this new way of experiencing, and given the fact that what gods are up to is endlessly creating, loving, and expanding, and having limitless curiosity, the project needed no promotion. It was announced, that is all, and billions of gods chose to participate.

XI.
Which Scenario
Gave Birth to the Other?

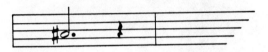

Maybe Scenario One came from Scenario Two and that is what this book is about: a nudge for you to remember who you are. You can remember any time you choose to remember. When you know you have experienced all the pain, agony, suffering, and effort you wanted, you can choose to remember.

XII.
Levels of Consciousness in Love

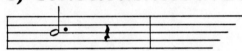

The arena of love is relationship: relationship to self and relationship to another, and finally, to others. The means, or tools to discover love of self, self-forgiveness, self-esteem, self-trust, and responsibility for your reality have been presented. Tools are useful only if they are used and no one can use them for you. The same tools can be used to expand your experience of loving and being loved by another, and ultimately to that love a god has for all his or her creations.

If one is seeking a relationship with one's self or with another as a goal, as an end, its achievement will be hollow and worthless. If one seeks relationship as a means to expand self-awareness, enrich understanding of the transcendent self, to explore the depths and breadths of the relationship, then there is no achieving, or attaining a final goal or state of being. There is only the eternal process of expanding the limits of responsibility and love—of growing, and becoming, and being.

There is an elemental, basic process which underlies all existence in the physical universe. It is that pattern or cycle through which all consciousness evolves. It is so fundamental to the existence of everything in the illusion-reality, so close to the core of creation, that it is almost invisible. Knowledge of this process is valueless as an end in itself. But when one uses that knowledge and understanding as a springboard to further evolution and growth, it becomes valuable.

It is a process of seven steps, stages, or levels, and the illusion of time itself derives from it. Since all time is simultaneous, there is no such process; therefore the process itself must be illusion, and it is. It is the made-up template for the growth of all things from sub-atomic to cosmic, from milli-seconds to trillions of years. It is one of those basic agreements or rules-of-the-game to which each of us agreed in order to play the game of being physical.

Rather than going through each of the seven levels, it is

easiest to look at the form of the whole process first:

Level 1 is that of total freedom and no responsibility; the conscious mind is not aware that it or the body is an individual, separate from the earth and sky—aware of no separation from nature. And, there is no awareness of being the cause of any of it; the question of "who causes it?" cannot arise.

Moving through levels 2 and 3 there is less and less freedom as the awareness of being separate from nature develops, until at level 4, there is no freedom and no responsibility. This is the level of 100% determinism: we are victims of each other and of our environment. The awareness of creating one's reality is zero.

Being in level 4 triggers the opportunity to move on to levels 5, 6 and 7.

Level 7 represents total freedom and total responsibility.

To move out of level 4 toward 5 requires the conscious choice to take back personal responsibility as the cause of, or creator of, one's reality. Eventually, all of us will make that choice since that is how we agreed to play this game. When you decide is up to you; there is plenty of time, all you want, as many lifetimes as you want. However—when you decide not to take back your personal power, you go back to level 1 and start over. This is why, in the preceding chapters, I have so often raised the issue of being bigger than your ego and your limiting beliefs, and have provided the tools for moving into level 5 and on out to total freedom, total responsibility.

Let us look at the seven process steps as applied to consciousness or awareness. It goes like this:

1. Mechanical awareness

2. Sensual awareness

3. Emotional awareness

4. Intellectual awareness—this is the pinnacle of domination by the ego; all cause seems to be outside the self. This does not mean that the intellect is wrong; it is ego and it is survival-dominated at this stage. No freedom and no responsibility.

5. Ideologic awareness: aware of something larger than the intellect; of being source or cause

6. Holistic awareness

7. Cosmic awareness—total freedom, total responsibility

Before discussing the process levels as related to relationship, let us look at why we are considering relationship at all. At any slice you might take through time, about one-third of the people in the world are satisfied being loners, and do not want intimate relationships. They may be pressured by their societies and shoved into relationships that they never wanted in the first place, however they do not want relationship. Another third wants to have multiple relationships, one after the other, or several going at the same time, and are content. And the other third want long-lasting monogamous relationships. None of these is better than another; none is more evolved, more right, healthier, etc. So if you are in one of these categories wishing to be in another and making where you are worse or better than another, relax. You are OK however you are about relationships. You can also change your mind and move into another category if you want to.

Now: what does the evolution of relationship, through the seven levels of process look like? When two people "relate," an entity called relationship is formed which is more than and different from the sum of the two participants. This entity begins in level 1 of process, that is, it is mechanical. We will examine what a loving, sexually intimate relationship of two people looks like as it moves through the levels. Time is not a limiting factor; that is, one could move through all levels in months or less, or take lifetimes. The same steps minus sexual intimacy could apply to intimate friendships.

LEVEL 1: MECHANICAL
(Explorative Demographic)

Before this level, the relationship has not existed in the physical reality, at least not consciously. Two people meet who have not met before and begin to interact. At this level there is complete freedom to interact or not, freedom to tell the truth or lie, and no responsibility for the relationship. Here the exchange of demographic information about each other begins: "What do you do?" "Where are you from?" "Who do you know that I know?," and so on. It is an exchange of facts or lies, of events and circumstances. Most of our acquaintances exist at this level, and even some whom you might consider friends, although that is stretching it a bit since no honesty, integrity, or responsibility exists here. It is all mechanical. Sexual exploration may start here or later.

LEVEL 2: SENSUAL
(Explorative Feeling)

This marks the beginning of the exchange of sensory data: what each likes and does not like—food, music, books, weather, sunsets, politics, parents, sex, whatever. Dissimilarities may stop the relationship, or may be put down on a mental scoreboard as minuses, or swept under the rug to be pulled out later as excuses or justifications. The ego is beginning to take over relationship: less freedom, no responsibility.

LEVEL 3: EMOTIONAL
(Explorative Spiritual)

This is reached when there begins to be an exchange of information related to emotions, with more intimacy; things hidden are revealed to the other, which results in a greater bonding between the two, or may end the relationship. If bonding occurs, there is less freedom. The stage is set for the next level. More and more each person is losing freedom; more and more there is dependence on the other person to determine one's emotional state. And of course the relationship does not depend on me, It depends on how the other person reacts to me and how I react to her or him.

LEVEL 4: INTELLECTUAL
(Static Intimacy)

Here, freedom is lost. Physical intimacy is at its peak in this relationship. This is the level very few have gone beyond, and it is the level we know how to attain. Our myths, stories, life-scripts, relationship courses, and therapies can get us to this level; or one can arrive here without benefit of the mass of intellectualization about it. We are experts at reaching this level. This is where the movie ends: man/woman gets woman/man and hangs on or loses. It is the same. But then what? What happened to living happily ever after? What happens after the joy or the tragedy at the end of the script?

Obviously, we have made a goal out of relating, and everything is supposed to work out once we have reached the goal of level 4.

It is "now that we have each other, we can turn our attention to jobs—families—other interests." That is exactly what happened when I "got" Jamie; now I could take my attention off the search, and turn it toward the "more important" areas of career, earning a living, making a contribution, etc. You saw what happened. Worse, you may decide that your relationship should have some higher purpose—some purpose bigger than itself. You get something bigger than the relationship, and the relationship shrinks, gets lost, and suffocates.

This level, although we have promoted it as the ideal, is actually static and stagnant intimacy. If it does not move to the next level, the relationship will go backward to three, two, one or zero, or from four to zero; one either starts over with someone else, or swears off relationships "forever." Time kills love in level 4.

Level 4 is the space in which falling in love or being in love with love happens in full flower. It can occur at any of the earlier levels, entirely in the imagination; but here it has all the support of our myths, love stories, music and poetry (ecstatic to despairing), and of society.

Dorothy Tennov, in her book LOVE AND LIMERENCE, The Experience of Being in Love, brilliantly describes this state of being for those of us who have experienced it, and for those who have not. But nearly everyone must have at least seen another in this state. She coined the word "limerence" to categorize this experience, or being in love with love or in love with experience of love, is about as far removed from the real experience of love as a human being can be. It represents the pinnacle of no freedom and no responsibility in relationship.

The person in limerence becomes the effect of the loved one. It is as though the limerent says, "I give you my life; I give you the responsibility for my joy and for my agony. Your loving attention fills me with hope and happiness. Your indifference or your neglect plunge me into fear and anguish."

In terms of the preceding chapters, the person in limerence becomes the victim of the "loved one," and then succumbs (sacrifices) to victimhood, or resists (sometimes with violence), or both.

If that were not enough, the person in limerence partially or wholly makes up—imagines—qualities and attributes of the "loved" one which do not exist in this reality. In Carl Jung's terms the attachment to a ghostly lover; a fiction superimposed on the body and name of the beloved.

People in full-blown limerence are unreal to their friends who are not in the same state. Their apparent happiness is fake: it does not communicate true emotion. Their despair and pain are relieved only by a smile, a phone call, or attention from the "loved" one.

> There is no medicine for Love,
> nor any charm,
> neither meat nor drink,
> but only kissing and embracing,
> and lying naked together.
>
> Daphnis et Chloe

When two people are in limerence with each other, they are both unreal to all others, and others are unreal to them. No communication is possible; words, yes, communication, no. And of course, each is, in part or wholly, making the other up; both in love with the perfect lover.

This state is the ego's masterpiece: a fraudulent imitation of what it thinks love is. Here it is very easy to see why the real experience of giving and receiving love requires responsibility for one's own reality, including responsibility for and willingness to communicate all emotion. The one in limerence would rather die than tell the "loved" one of the pain, fear, grief, and anger he or she experiences—all out of the fear of losing him or her. The limerent never notices that the one certain way to lose a lover is to hide one's feelings and emotions. Here we have the extreme example of the two major barriers to the experience and expression of love: victimhood and suppression of emotion.

The way out, of course, is to take the lid off one's suppressed feelings, and this can lead to the realization of responsibility.

The following paragraphs are essential to an understanding of the interrelationship between the two major barriers, and to everything else in this book so far:

When emotions are expressed to another without the experience of responsibility for the circumstance which gave rise to the emotions, damage occurs to the self-esteem of both members of a relationship, and the expressed emotion does not disappear. It becomes a resentment or a regret. This is one of the reasons we have been so carefully taught to suppress ourselves emotionally.

Most of us died emotionally between the ages of zero and six. We tried to express emotions to mother, father, or their surrogates, and found that our feelings had little or no impact. We viewed our parents as always right, so when mother said "Don't be afraid!" we decided there was something wrong with being afraid, and tried to suppress fear, or at least not let anyone know about it. And to tell mother or father we were afraid of them would be nearly unthinkable. Sadness and grief were somewhat understood, and might get some sympathy.

But anger! It seemed to have no impact at all. Worse, we were afraid that if either parent really understood how angry we were at either or both of them, they would stop loving us, punish us, send us away, or even flush us down the toilet. The suppressed anger of the child is rarely expressed, even in adolescence. Here the anger is righteous, judgmental, and punishing, and does not release the anger which the child and adolescent feel they have no right to express. This becomes guilt and depression, then apathy, then death.

The key to the release of the emotions is this: the emotion must be recognized and expressed first, from the responsible position of: "Yes—I am angry at you for . . . and my expression of it does not mean that this is the end of our relationship. I know that if I do not express it, it will result in the end of our relationship."

Then, after it is expressed, you can take further responsibility by asking yourself, "Why? Why was I angry? And why was I angry at that?" Asking why will lead you to full responsibility and to the fear which underlies the anger.

Then, process the fear: "Why am I afraid? Why am I afraid of that?"

For the person receiving the anger, the responsible process would be to look into the angry person's reality (empathy) and see whether what you did was an intentional attack, and then ask why you did that.

And then to finish it off; "What feelings do I have—how do I feel now that I have released and taken responsibility for the anger and the fear?"

It is only when emotions are expressed against the backdrop or context of responsibility, that the emotion is released, disappears, and the flow of love which was always there is revealed. It does little good for a group of people to get together and spill their feelings about each other all over the place if there is no awareness of responsibility: no awareness that each of us creates his or her own reality, and that the reality we each create includes all the people we interact with—in short, everyone. And further, your anger has no impact on a bed or a table, and if it is deflected or misdirected to a person other than the real object of the anger, it is damaging to the self-esteem of the person who receives it, and you are left with it being unreleased, unrecreated by another.

Limerence varies widely in its intensity and duration. People can actually remain in that state over a lost lover for lifetimes. There are persons around longing for their soul mate. As we will see later, there is no soul mate. If there were, he or she would not be lost. Soul mates are created, not found. You do not have one waiting for you or hiding from you on earth or in the great beyond.

I am not saying or implying that all people in process level 4 experience limerence. Not at all. Real love is the basis of relationship for many in level 4. I have emphasized limerence as the extreme example of no conscious responsibility and conscious suppression of emotion. Also, real love does not disappear in the limerent experience; it just gets buried alive and does not die.

How can you recognize the real thing?

1.   Love is giving 100% and receiving 100%. That is, giving all the love you have to give without expectation or need for love to be returned; and receiving with 100% of your capability.

2.   It is trusting, with no testing.

3.   It is bringing your full self-esteem to the relationship, and never intentionally damaging the self-esteem of another. If you depend on others for your self-esteem you experience neither love nor self-esteem. It is transcending the ego's requirement for outside validation. The ego will say, "People will know I am alright when they see me with or know about my relationship with this wonderful person; and I know I must be alright if such a wonderful person loves me." If you find yourself saying that to yourself, then it is your ego or survival beliefs which are running your love affair, not you. The voice in your head which

needs outside validation as the source of self-esteem is coming from your child, an earlier you who does and always will require the approval or praise of others, or their envy, to prove that you are worthy. Listen to the voice of your child, and if you would experience love, do not make those childish beliefs your own. Love the child; you, the adult, can supply all the outside validation the child needs, and his or her own voice of fear will no longer spill over into your reality.

4.   It is the preference to need another. It is not need out of fear or loneliness or seeking protection, but need freely chosen by two individuals absolutely secure in their own self-trust and fully aware of their own self-worth.

5.   It is allowing it to happen: allowing the relationship to unfold. It is not forcing issues, demanding decisions; it is not making the relationship happen or be cast in a form. It is letting it happen in the gradualness of time. It is taking your hands off the wheel.

Within the last three weeks, I have experienced what this chapter is about: it started when it looked like the one I loved (with some limerence) was being dishonest with me. I had to ask myself the following question: "If my reality is reflecting dishonesty, how am I being dishonest?"

The answer came loud and clear. I was withholding my feelings and emotions from him—my hurt, my anger, my fear. In an explosive and still partly irresponsible state, I took the lid off, expressed it all. He was hurt, confused, and had the greatness and love to say so.

Then, I proposed the following, which seemed rational, logical, and justifiable: I said, "What I want is a permanent monogamous relationship with you. If your answer is 'yes,' that will be great; and if it is 'no,' that will be great too. I am going to leave you for a few days. I see how I have smothered you. But please give me your answer when I come back. I love you."

He cried.

I did leave town, and after a few days I saw what I had done. First, I had seen only two possible answers to my proposal: yes or no. And with that, I gave him the responsibility of determining my future; I was asking him to steer the boat. Worse, since he loved me and did not want to commit himself now to a permanent relationship, it looked to him like he would lose each way: if he said yes, he would be doing something he felt forced into, if he said no, he would lose me.

When I had seen all that I returned. We had lunch and I told him what I had done, and apologized. And perhaps most important of all, I had forgiven myself, and saw my mistake for what all mistakes are, as an opportunity for a breakthrough.

What happened at that lunch cannot be put completely into words. Suddenly all the heaviness in our relationship disappeared for both of us, and we were free to love each other without conditions or strings or forms. For me the shift was from a passionate attachment to him, to a compassionate detachment. He was relieved of a burden I had tried to force on him—that of being responsible for my life. Now the relationship is in a place I have never experienced before: loving, compassionate, and free. It is unfolding. And there is a depth of intimacy and empathy I did not know was possible.

You can check yourself with the list above. These are pre-requisites, for making the quantum leap to level 5 (Pages 126–127).

To restate a condition I mentioned earlier: one cannot remain in level 4 of process. One either goes ahead, or slips back down to level 1 or zero.

Level 4 can be maintained for a time, even a long time if you are aware of where you are and choose not to go on. But it will reverse without the mutual desire of two peole to explore the real depth and breadth of relationship, and to process all emotions.

LEVEL 5: IDEOLOGIC
(Passionate Intimacy)

Level 5 is usually frightening. This is where most people would rather ". . . pass out of love's threshing floor into the seasonless world . . ." Some couples step into it, have a taste of it, then back off out of fear. It is too good to be true. I do not desire it. I will lose my precious freedom (not noticing that you never had any). You gave up freedom when you set limits for yourself and gave away your responsibility for your reality. A caged animal is not free. Neither is a caged human being.

This is the beginning of ecstasy. It requires total letting go. That is frightening. It scares the hell out of the ego. It screams: "NO!! YOU SHALL REMAIN SEPARATE! SEPARATE YOU WERE BORN AND SEPARATE YOU SHALL REMAIN— FOREVER!!" This level requires monogamy, and monogamy by choice: by two people willing to bring their own self-love and self-esteem and trust and 100% giving and receiving love to each other freely and joyfully, just because they will it to be so, and not because of an agreed-on form for the relationship.

This could best be called the level of explorative passionate intimacy. Monogamy is important for many reasons, not the least of which is the fact that when you have intercourse with another, you carry for three weeks the vibrational energy of the person with whom you had intercourse: their negative as well as their positive vibrational energy. You are no longer just yourself. Orgasm greatly intensifies this effect.

When sexual expression of love occurs in the context of monogamy, an empathy and compassion for the other occurs such that each partner knows, without words or even proximity, what is happening, often in detail, with the other. There is an expanded experience of love.

If one partner in a monogamous relationship has intercourse with someone outside the relationship, that partner now carries the "outsider's" energy—positive and negative—for three weeks, so powerful is the bonding of the two personalities. One is no longer just oneself, but the other as well. It is confusing and dissonant since there will be unfamiliar and unexplained thoughts, feeling, emotional states, and somtimes illness. And the monogamous partner will be confused too. Worse, if the "outsider" is jealous, or has the intent to break up the monogamous relationship, the relationship suffers severe stress and strain, and neither partner may be able to understand why.

I am not discussing this problem as a moral or ethical issue. It is simply another barrier to the experience of love for which, if recognized, one can take responsibility.

To deny or inhibit orgasm is to deny oneself or others the most direct and powerful communion with one's higher self that is available to most human beings. The experience is outside of time; there is no ego; no physical limitations; and in that timeless moment there can be the experience of absolute love, and union, fusion, with the other. When there is guilt about orgasm or sex; when one is using sex as a weapon to dominate another by force, or to punish another by withholding it; or for the purpose of inflicting pain, or to gain self-esteem, this com-munion occurs, but cannot be recognized. And we damage our-selves equally or more than the damage we inflict on others, out of our natural integrity—the intention of the Self, or who you are, to not inflict damage.

We gave ourselves bodies with sex organs to have fun with, to use as vehicles or means for understanding our true nature; for a natural and transcendent symbol of the communication of love. Used for the ego's reasons, and to validate our negative be-liefs, there is not much fun, and little or no communication of love. I include masturbation in this discussion: it can be used as a beautiful and powerful expression of self-love, or as a guilt-producing demonstration of self-hate. How you use sex is up to you. Even some so-called sado-masochistic practices and tech-niques may serve as expressions of love, or as vicious expres-sions of resentments and suppressed emotions.

Monogamy is not a requirement of level 4. Even with mon-ogamy, people in the fourth level will regress with respect to relationship unless the choice is made to take responsibility, to grow, to give up the childish and adolescent games of victim-hood, negative ego, manipulation, and hurting each other. Only that decision will allow the relationship to move out of the state of no freedom and no responsibility, heading toward freedom, with responsibility.

So monogamy is required, and something else equally threatening to the ego is required: there must be freely chosen total and mutual commitment to the relationship, such that it, the relationship, takes priority over everything else: over the jobs, projects, social activities, everything. And over all other relationships.

Now, herein lies a paradox. People in level 5 are so rare that almost no one knows that if the relationship is nurtured and loved, everything else begins to work naturally, effortlessly, with joy and celebration.

Briefly, the last two levels are:

LEVEL 6: HOLISTIC (Explorative compassionate
intimacy)

LEVEL 7: COSMIC (Eternal intimacy, free and
together by choice forever)

Soul mates are not found. They are created by you out of total responsibility, freedom, love, and hard work. Hard work does not mean that it is not fun.

Be honest with yourself, especially with respect to your emotions. Allowed, experienced, expressed, the free flow of the spiral of emotions will lead you with certainty toward unconditional love and the self-esteem and self-love which are revealed by taking responsibility.

You will have regained those absolute qualities of godliness which you gave up, temporarily, in order to be human.

In the beginning of this book I said that you will not find the truth written in these or any other pages. As in Sir Edward Elgar's ENIGMA VARIATIONS (specifically, and other great music generally) there is an unstated theme which is the context —the truth. Each of us can discover it, and when you do, you know who you are, but cannot state it. Contexts cannot be communicated in words; only implied. In Richard Bach's words, "But remember, . . . that not being known doesn't stop the truth from being true."*

One final clue: we do live in separate realities, in the illusion. The boundaries of our separate illusion-realities are inviolate. As we communicate our experience to each other, we can have glimpses and views of the landscapes of another's illusion-

*THERE'S NO SUCH PLACE AS FAR AWAY: Bach, Richard;
Delacorte Press/Eleanor Friede; 1979.

reality, but the boundaries remain inviolate.

As we communicate our experience, and open ourselves to receiving the experience of others, we come closer to transcending the boundaries of our separate realities.

The one absolute quality which empowers us to transcend those boundaries is Love.

FINALE

This is an unfinished symphony, as all symphonies and books must finally be. It has no second or third or fourth movement. You are the last movement and the first and all between. A symphony or a book or a poem or a painting is not an end of and to itelf, but a beginning: a springboard from which, if you choose, you can propel yourself beyond limits and boundaries, all of which you have ever so carefully built up around yourself.

This little book wrote itself for me. As I was writing some of the more dramatic parts, I experienced my life up to now as a long movie which I wrote. If I carry the memories of it around with me it is not different from walking out of a theater, having been engrossed in the drama, carrying that memory around for an hour or so, then letting it go. I have let it all go. You can too.

I have thanked all the members of my cast for playing their roles perfectly. I know that it was a gift of love. Now it is time for a new script, or perhaps, no script at all. Whether there is a scenario or not, I know it will never end. There are only beginnings.

It's just the beginning—what wonders await you!
Nourish the love that grows stronger each moment;
Never despair if the pathway seems troubled:
All is forgiven. Empowered by your lovelights,
Together forever, you stand at the threshold of
Blessed creation: the two of you joyously, recklessly,
Boundlessly romping
Through spaces and magnitudes, endlessly soaring.
Love and creation, linked ever together,
Propel you to glories beyond understanding . . .